Bride Arise

Geoff Woodcock

onewith**christ**.org

Jesus—You are my beloved, and I am Yours.

Unless otherwise stated, English definitions of Greek and Hebrew words are taken from the *HELPS Lexicon* as published within *The Discovery Bible* software, available at thediscoverybible.com.

Unless otherwise stated, all Scripture quotations are taken from *The ESV Bible* (The Holy Bible, English Standard Version), copyright © 2001 by Crossway, a publishing ministry of Good News Publishers. Used by permission. All rights reserved.

Scripture quotations marked (NASB) are taken from *The New American Standard Bible* ® (1995 Update) Copyright ©1960, 1962, 1963, 1968, 1971, 1972, 1973, 1975, 1977, 1995 by the Lockman Foundation. Used by permission. All rights reserved.

Scripture quotations marked (NKJV) are taken from *The New King James Version*, ©1979, 1980, 1982 by Thomas Nelson, Inc. Used by permission. All rights reserved.

Scripture quotations marked (BSB) are taken from *The Berean Study Bible New Testament*, - copyright © 2016, Bible Hub (Biblehub.com). Used by permission. All rights reserved.

Scripture quotations marked (NLT) are taken from the *Holy Bible: New Living Translation*. Wheaton, Ill: Tyndale House Publishers, copyright © 2004. Used by permission. All rights reserved.

Scripture quotations marked (TDB) are taken from *The Discovery Bible,* copyright © 2018, HELPS Ministries Inc. Used by permission. All rights reserved.

Thanks to Brian Upsher for editorial support, and to Nikki Miller, Donna Nichol, and Suzanne Lewis for proofing. And of course, thanks to my wife Melanie, without whom this book would not have been possible.

Bride Arise by Geoff Woodcock

Book Two of the *One with Christ Series*

Revision 2, January 2021

ISBN: 978-0-9951408-1-3

ISSN: 2624-411X

Published by Acacia Media | www.acacia.media

Printed in the United States of America

Other Formats

978-0-9951207-8-5 (PDF)

978-0-9951408-2-0 (Kindle)

978-0-9951207-9-2 (ePub)

This book is available free online at www.onewithchrist.org

Contents

Introduction

Matthew 5:6

"Blessed are those who hunger and thirst for righteousness, for they shall be satisfied."

Hunger is a blessing that few people want, yet it is one of the most powerful blessings we can receive. In the natural realm, starving people have a single, unwavering focus: *food*. Their hunger removes every distraction and motivates them to sacrifice anything to get the food they so desperately need.

This principle is also true in our spiritual lives. When we are hungry for Jesus, our hunger dissolves the distractions of the world. Like the blind men on the side of the road, our hunger makes us cry out to Jesus as He passes by. And Jesus always stops for the cry of the hungry. This makes hunger one of the most powerful keys to spiritual growth.

Day after day, the incredible blessings of God pass us by as we busy ourselves with the affairs of life. If we want to take hold of these blessings, we need to become truly hungry for Him. This is especially true when we look at the blessings that God is offering us in this book. People do not casually drift into a wholehearted love for Jesus. Experiencing the love of the bride and the Bridegroom requires a resolve that only comes with hunger and humility.[1]

So are you hungry? Do you long for a greater experience of God? Are you searching for something real? Are you willing to invest time in getting to know God more? If so, then get ready for the greatest adventure you will ever have!

Love is not a theory to be learned, but a spiritual reality to be experienced. So I encourage you to take time to connect with the Holy Spirit as you read this book. He can change us more in a single encounter than we could ever change ourselves with years of learning. With this in mind, each chapter ends with a short prayer to help you remain connected to the Holy Spirit as you read. At the end of the book is a Study Guide that contains some questions and reflection exercises for each chapter. These are designed to help you to commune more deeply with the Holy Spirit by giving Him space to speak to you, to share His heart with you, and to fill you with His love. Many people have had incredible encounters with God as they have done the reflections, so I invite you to invest time in them.

Journey of Love

Our whole spiritual life is a journey of relationship with God. Whether we are aware of it or not, all the steps of this journey into love, from the first to last, are ordered by God and taken with Him. As you start out, be prepared for a quiet battle. We have an enemy that is determined to keep us from experiencing the awesome love of God, and one of the most effective weapons he uses is distraction. So ask God to help you to be sensitive to potential distractions and deal with them early. Time is short, and we do not want to be delayed.[2]

> **1 Corinthians 13:2b**
> ...if I have all faith, so as to remove mountains, but have not love, I am nothing.

At the outset, it is important to note that we can receive revelation, attain knowledge, and even have the faith to move mountains; but if we lack love then it is all in vain. Without love we are nothing and can do nothing. Therefore as we begin this journey with God, we need to know that it is love alone that gives this journey meaning. And because we grow in love through every step, our goal is not only found in the destination, but in the journey itself. The journey to love is a journey of love.

This book builds on the foundation that is laid in *First Love*, the first book in the *One with Christ* series. Any essential material from *First Love* is briefly summarised in this book where needed, but if you would like to read *First Love*, it is available for free online at www.onewithchrist.org

Please note that I have been careful not to exaggerate nor embellish the testimonies in this book, but to accurately recount them to the best of my memory. At the time of publishing, I believe all the people involved in the testimonies are still alive and can bear witness to their truth.

Thank you for taking this journey into love. I am incredibly excited for you and look forward to meeting you in eternity and hearing all about it! May God continually pour out His love, faith, grace, humility and joy over you as you walk with Him, and may you grow more and more into your awesome design of love and unity with Jesus.

Geoff (Jeff) Woodcock

Prologue

When I saw her, I was 24 years old. I had been following Jesus since my teens, but the moment I looked into her eyes, my life, my faith, and my relationship with God were changed forever.

To me she was the picture of ideal beauty. No makeup. No jewellery. Just unaccented, exquisite beauty. Yet it was not her outward appearance that captured my heart. It was her eyes. I looked into her eyes and I could see into her soul. And she was beautiful.

When our eyes met, an unexpected wave of love washed over me and soaked into me. As she held my gaze, her eyes radiated such an exclusive and intense love for me that for that moment the world dissolved around me and there existed only love. The wave of love that had so completely saturated me then receded back to her. As it returned, it drew every last measure of love out of me. With just a look, she had both filled me and drained me. I was overwhelmed, exhilarated, and utterly undone.

It was my time for love. But as quickly as she had appeared, she was gone, having taken my heart with her. I was left alone and breathless, with two questions.

"My God, who is this woman? And where is she?"

Before I could discover the truth of who this woman was and how she came to possess such a powerful love, there was a journey I had to take. The first step of that journey was to consciously devote myself to the pursuit of love.

Before we go on, it may be useful to know a little of my background in terms of love. Love did not come easily to me. My upbringing was largely void of affection and emotional intimacy. I have no recollection of being embraced by my mother and my father hugged me only twice: once after I was baptised at the age of 16, and again when I left home to attend university.

The perceived lack of love in my upbringing did not leave me with any sense of self-pity but rather the belief that I did not need love. I resolved that my experience would become my strength rather than my weakness. After all, love was not needed to make friends or find success. I could still follow God and lead a fulfilling life without it. I did not consciously envy people who were seeking love or who had found love. Rather, I reasoned that other people needed love to make up for a weakness in their character or to fill an emotional gap they had allowed to appear in their soul. But not me. I was a strong, determined, and self-sufficient follower of Christ.

In my second year of university, my mentor came to me with what I think he believed was a word from God.

"You will find love," he told me.

"I don't need love. It's not important for me." I was quick to dismiss the word, but he persisted.

"You will find love," he insisted. Even after all our times talking together, I realised that he still did not know me that well.

"I have never had love. I have learned to live without it. If I needed love, God would have given it to me. He didn't, so clearly I don't need it."

"You will find love," he repeated.

"I don't think you understand. It's not for me. It's for other people, but love is not for me."

Neither one of us was making any progress, so I left and spent some time in a park quietly rethinking my perspective on love. The obvious contradiction of believing that I needed God, but did not need love, never occurred to me. It just seemed so unbelievable that someone would truly love me that I simply could not bring myself to trust love in other people. I told myself that most young women are insecure and that they express affection only because of their need to find security in others. I was cynical, naïve, and emotionally impaired. I did not believe in love and had no vision for love at all. I could not even say what genuine love may look like. But on that day in the park I reached a turning point. I opened my heart to the possibility of change and left it all in the hands of God. He could do as He liked, and I would try not to resist Him. I walked out of the park and without a word, the Spirit of God went to work in me.

Over the next few years, my heart was slowly softened to love. I started to understand a little more of the love of God and even desire that love. Something was changing.

After a year or so, I heard a person teach from the Song of Songs. He said that the love of God was intoxicating like a strong wine. I had reached the point where this idea of love was both attractive and confronting. For while I could say that God loved me, I could not honestly say that I had experienced His intoxicating love. In my mind, I knew God loved me, but my heart was still far from addicted.

I was honest with God and admitted that I was not intoxicated with the love of Jesus. But I wanted to be. The desire was finally present in me to experience this kind of love. So I asked Jesus to overwhelm me with His love. After that prayer, my experience of love continued to grow. Then a year later, I saw her.

The woman who looked into my eyes so captivated me with her love appeared in a vision. We shared a single moment and then she vanished, leaving me with an incredible gift from God: a lasting revelation of divine love. That vision launched me into a journey of the instruction, experience, and transformation of love. It was a journey into the heart of God and into a love that redefined my identity and determined my purpose in the world. And it is a journey I would like to take you on.

I know that in the beginning this may sound like we are starting out on a bit of a fairy-tale. It can be hard to believe that such a love exists. But it does. I saw the vision and then found the reality—I have been there and I know the way. And now I would like to invite you to take the first step.

When you are ready, take a breath, say a prayer, and turn the page.

1 | Design of Love

We are about to set out on a journey, and like all journeys, the best way to start is by setting our compass in the right direction. In this case, our goal is not simply to have an experience of God's love but to forge a whole new identity of love with Him.

In *First Love,* we explored the connection between identity and purpose. Our identity is our sense of *who* we are, and our purpose is our sense of *why* we are. As we grow up, we form an identity for ourselves which then shapes our entire lives. Our belief about who we are determines the value we place on our own lives. It affects the decisions we make, the friends we choose, the interests we invest in, the work we pursue and so on. If we have a broken sense of identity, we often make poor choices that can end up sabotaging our own lives. So how do we come to a true sense of our identity?

In the natural realm, identity always builds upon purpose. We see this in the things people make. Our lives are filled with inventions, and each one is designed to fulfil a certain purpose. Houses are designed to shelter us, cars to transport us, ovens to cook food, cameras to take photos, and so on. We always relate to our inventions based on their purpose, which is why we never expect a washing machine to cook our dinner or to entertain us. Rather, we know that the value of every invention is only found in its ability to function according to its design.

Defining Design

All creation finds its greatest joy when it is living according to its design. So like a fish being returned to the water, our journey into design comes with a restoration of joy—not the fleeting high of a feel-good moment, but the sustained satisfaction found in getting life right. So what is our design?

The purpose of every invention comes solely from the mind of its creator. We would not build an intelligent washing machine and then give it the freedom to define its own purpose in life. Otherwise it could start to believe it was a freezer, only to get frustrated as it tries but fails to freeze our clothes. Instead, we would make its purpose clear. This would set our creation free to discover its true identity and experience its greatest joy.

This principle applies to all creation. Because nothing made itself, nothing has the right to define its own purpose in life. That privilege belongs only to the Creator. And this applies especially to us. Because God created us, we do not have the right to define our own purpose or identity. Instead, if we want to know who we are and why we exist, we need to ask the One who made us.

James 1:23-25

For if anyone is a hearer of the word and not a doer, he is like a man who looks intently at his natural face in a mirror. For he looks at himself and goes away and at once forgets what he was like. But the one who looks into the perfect law, the law of liberty, and perseveres, being no hearer who forgets but a doer who acts, he will be blessed in his doing.

Scripture speaks of the word of God being like a mirror. In the same way that a physical mirror shows us who we are physically, the word of God is a spiritual mirror that shows us who we are spiritually. As we learn to read the Bible as a mirror, we find that the Scriptures not only reveal who God is, but they also reveal who we are. Through the Scriptures, God reveals our design, purpose and identity in life.

At the Beginning

Psalm 119:68

You are good and do good; teach me your statutes.

Genesis 1:31

And God saw everything that he had made, and behold, it was very good. And there was evening and there was morning, the sixth day.

In the beginning, God created everything according to His perfect plan. So what was God's creation like? At the end of each of the first five days of creation, Scripture says God looked and "saw that it was good." On the sixth day, God created people in His image. He looked again and saw that it was *very* good. Over and over Scripture draws attention to the goodness of creation. Why? Because God does what He is. God is good and He invests His goodness in His creation. The same principle is true of God's love: God is love and does love. Therefore, when God created us, He made us as living expressions of His love and goodness. He did not make us to be servants, tirelessly serving the wants of our master. On the contrary, God created us to be good people who radiate His love.

The Greatest Command

Matthew 22:34-40 (BSB)

And when the Pharisees heard that Jesus had silenced the Sadducees, they themselves gathered together. One of them, an expert in the law, tested Him with a question: "Teacher, which commandment is the greatest in the Law?"

Jesus declared, "'Love the Lord your God with all your heart and with all your soul and with all your mind.' This is the first and greatest commandment. And the second is like it: 'Love your neighbour as yourself.' All the Law and the Prophets depend on these two commandments.'"

In *First Love,* we looked at design in terms of a clockmaker creating a clock. If the clockmaker was to give one command to the clock, it would simply be: *Tell the time.* Through this one command, the clockmaker makes the entire purpose of the clock clear. Jesus does exactly the same thing here. By giving us one single command, Jesus beautifully reveals God's purpose for our lives. Every one of us has been perfectly designed by God to love Him with all our heart, soul, mind and strength. We all have completely unique personalities and callings, but we are all bound together by this inescapable truth: God has perfectly made every part of our being to come alive with love.

This design of love has been proven by science. When people experience selfless love, their brains light up with activity and release hormones that bring about a sense of joy, warmth, fulfilment, peace and well-being. In the absence of love, our brains suffer damage. Babies and elderly people often die without love. At every stage of life, we need love, and if we fail to find it, we so often turn to distraction and addiction. All the problems within our families, communities, and nations stem from this lack of love. But it does not have to stay this way. If we are willing to go to the root of our brokenness, God can heal us, our families, our communities, and even entire nations. God has the answer and it is found in our amazing design of love.

Essential Unity

But is it actually possible to love God with our entire being? Can anyone attain this kind of life? Can we overcome our own selfishness and fill our hearts with love? No! God alone is love and this life of wholehearted love is entirely impossible outside Christ. But we are not outside Christ. We are *in* Christ Jesus and He is *in* us.

> **2 Corinthians 13:5**
> Examine yourselves, to see whether you are in the faith. Test yourselves. Or do you not realise this about yourselves, that Jesus Christ is in you?—unless indeed you fail to meet the test!

> **Ephesians 3:14-17a**
> For this reason I bow my knees before the Father, from whom every family in heaven and on earth is named, that according to the riches of his glory he may grant you to be strengthened with power through his Spirit in your inner being, so that Christ may dwell in your hearts through faith...

Our design of love can only be found in union with Jesus. He lives within us, and He wants to live through us. When we look through the lens of unity, we see that all the commands of Scripture refer to a life of unity with Jesus. We are called to love God with all our hearts because Jesus loves the Father with all His heart. Scripture tells us to be righteous because Jesus is righteous.[1] We are to be humble and gentle because Jesus is humble and gentle.[2] Scripture calls us to love fervently because Jesus wants to love fervently through us.[3] We are to be holy because Jesus is holy and He wants to share His holiness with us.[4] Through every command, God is not calling us to *like* Jesus but to be one with Jesus.

> **Deuteronomy 30:6,11** (NASB)
> "Moreover the LORD your God will circumcise your heart and the heart of your descendants, to love the LORD your God with all your heart and with all your soul, in order that you may live...
>
> "For this commandment that I command you today is not too hard for you, neither is it far off."

Here God promises that if we will choose to love Him with all our heart and soul, He will do whatever it takes to make it a reality. He will transform our hearts and fill us with the life of Christ so that we can live in His design of love. He is God and He can do it.

Reality Guaranteed

I recently saw God fulfil this promise in a glorious way. I was part of a team that was visiting a Pakistani refugee community. Most of the people there had left Pakistan seeking asylum, only to be denied by the UN. We went with a heart to bless these people, connect, and listen to their stories. One man told us how he shared a book in his church that included a section which promoted educating women. The Taliban found out and put a death-warrant on him, forcing him to flee the country. Another man in the community had been shot twice and left for dead before being helped to recover and escape.

Another couple, whom we will call Daniel and Sarah, invited us to have a dinner at their place.[5] Sarah was one of the most radiant people I have ever met. She was glowing with a tangible sense of love and joy. Over the course of dinner, we asked Sarah to share her story. Why had she fled Pakistan?

"My life is a bit like a movie. When I was 15, I was engaged to Daniel [for a future marriage], but that year, my mother died. When I was 17, my father died as well. My uncles wanted the house, so they took our inheritance and forced me and my two younger sisters to leave and live with an aunt. One day, a Muslim man came to my aunt and offered her $300 to buy me as a second wife. My aunt agreed and sold me to the man. He took me by force to his home and handcuffed me to a chain. The man and his wife took all my clothes. Then they broke both my feet.

"I suffered greatly over that time. They would often torture me and rape me. They would force me to work in the house and they would starve me of food. After seven years, the man told me that I had to become a Muslim or he would kill me. His plan was to cut up my body and throw the pieces in the river. I refused and said, 'Jesus has not given up on me, so I will not give up on Jesus. Kill me if you like, but I will not become a Muslim.' While the man and his wife were away, his brother came to me and said, 'You must become Muslim. He is returning tomorrow to kill you if you will not convert.' I still refused and so he said, 'If you're not going to become a Muslim then you had better run.' He then unlocked my chains and I fled. I could barely walk, but I made it to the next village and then the one beyond. It was a miracle, but I found Daniel. It had been over seven years since we last saw each other, but he had not married anyone else. In fact, he had been looking for me!

"Even though I had been a sex slave, Daniel said to me, 'I don't care what's happened to you. God chose you to be my wife and we will get married and have a future together.' I was so thankful. We got married, but the man who kept me captive was still seeking to kill me, so we fled the country."

Our translator explained that when they arrived in the new country, Sarah and Daniel went through the asylum-seeking process, but were denied asylum, presumably because Sarah could not prove her slavery or the threat against her life. So they had been living in hiding for the last six years. Sarah then continued her story.

"For the last six years, I have struggled with rage, depression, bitterness, grief and pain. But then a friend gave me a copy of *Bride Arise* in Urdu. As I was reading it, Jesus became so real for me! I gave my whole heart to loving Him, and He kept coming to me and filling me with His love. His love has healed me! This is the first time I've been able to talk about my past without crying. In fact, when I think of my time in slavery, I can't feel any pain in the memory! I can't even feel the slightest bit of resentment towards the man who enslaved and tortured me for all those years! All I can feel is the love and joy of Jesus! In fact, I would go through all that slavery again just to have this love for Jesus!"

Our team was both humbled and awestruck. Despite having endured so much, Sarah had chosen to embrace her design of love, and this choice gave God the permission He needed to make it a reality. In keeping with His promise, God had perfectly healed her heart and consumed her with His love. And it showed. Sarah was literally beaming with the love and joy of Christ. Knowing that they have so little, I asked Sarah if there was anything she needed or if we could help in any way. She looked at me with a puzzled expression, as if to say, *Haven't you been listening?* She simply replied, "The only thing I need is more love for Jesus!"

God promises us: if we seek a life of wholehearted love and unity with Jesus, He will make it happen. He will break our chains, heal our hearts, and fill us with His love. Let us choose His love today!

Pray

Father, thank you for promising to make it possible for me to live a life of wholehearted love. Please help me to take the next steps in this direction.

2 | Channels of Love

As awe-inspiring as God's design of love and unity with Jesus is, there are greater depths still to explore. In order to discover more of the riches of our design, we need to look back before the beginning of time and creation.

John 17:24
"Father, I desire that they also, whom You have given Me, be with Me where I am, so that they may see My glory which You have given Me, for You loved Me before the foundation of the world."

Before the universe was created and the foundations of the world were laid, the Father loved the Son. And long after our world ends, the Father will still love the Son. This flow of love between the Father and Son is the ultimate, overarching reality in all eternity.

Our universe occupies only a small moment within eternity, and so all of creation is set in the context of this eternal flow of love between the Father and the Son. *This includes us.* If we are to discover our place in creation, we need to see our lives in the light of the divine flow of love between the Father and the Son.

The Father's Love for Jesus

In *First Love,* we spent some time reflecting on the Father's love for Jesus. This is worth doing regularly as we grow in Christ. So before we go on, let us take a moment to ask the Father for a fresh insight into His love for Jesus. Let the Holy Spirit inspire your imagination, open the eyes of your heart, and help you catch a vision of the Father's love for Jesus. Take a few minutes to let it settle in your heart and then come back and continue reading.

What words could possibly describe the Father's love for Jesus? It is beautiful, powerful, and passionate far beyond all description. It is all-consuming in its intensity and perfect in purity. It is a love that surpasses all comprehension; all we can hope for is to be overwhelmed by a fleeting glimpse of the eternal love that is shared between the Father and the Son.

John 15:9
"As the Father has loved me, so have I loved you. Abide in my love."

John 17:22-23 (NLT)
"I have given them the glory you gave me, so they may be one as we are one. I am in them and you are in me. May they experience such perfect unity that the world will know that you sent me and that you love them as much as you love me."

Before even reading these verses, a friend shared an experience she had when meditating on the Father's love for Jesus.

"I don't get many visions from the Lord. But when I asked the Father what His love for Jesus is like, He took me into a vision. I was surrounded on every side with the most incredible explosions of energy and light. It was like there were explosions on top of explosions. It was intense. Then the Father spoke to me and said, 'This is just a fraction of how much I love Jesus, and I love you in exactly the same way!'"

Only when we have a sense of the Father's love for Jesus can we begin to understand how much we are loved. Both of the passages above use the Greek word *kathos,* meaning to the same extent; fully corresponding to; or exactly equivalent. Jesus loves us in exactly the same way as the Father loves Him. And the Father loves us just as much as He loves Jesus. As incredible as it sounds, both the Father and Son love us with the same infinite, eternal, consuming, passionate love that they have for each other. There are no degrees of love with God. He always loves in the extreme and He has set His love upon us. We are loved by God more than we could ever imagine.

For Jesus

Colossians 1:15-17

He [Jesus] is the image of the invisible God, the firstborn of all creation. For by him all things were created, in heaven and on earth, visible and invisible, whether thrones or dominions or rulers or authorities—all things were created through him and for him. And he is before all things, and in him all things hold together.

The Father created all things through Jesus and *for* Jesus. From the smallest grain of sand to the greatest star in the universe—all of creation is a gift from the Father to Jesus. *This includes us.* We were not made for ourselves, rather the Father created us to be living gifts of His love for Jesus. And God does not give defective gifts to His Son. Each one of us has been wonderfully made by the Father to express His love for Jesus.

We can see this clearly in the words of Jesus' final prayer.

John 17:25-26 (BSB)

"Righteous Father, although the world has not known You, I know You, and they know that You sent Me. And I have made Your name known to them and will continue to make it known, so that the love You have for Me may be in them, and I in them."

Imagine your final prayer before you die. Who would you pray for and what would you pray?

Here Jesus is praying to the Father for all believers throughout the ages, including you. In His final words of prayer before the cross, Jesus prays His greatest desire and in doing so, He reveals the Father's ultimate plan for our creation. The Father sent Jesus to make His true nature known to His people *so that* the Father's love for Jesus could live in us.

Read verse 26 again. *"And I have made Your name known to them and will continue to make it known, so that the love You have for Me may be in them, and I in them."*

Read it slowly and let the words burn into your heart: **The Father's love for Jesus can live in us**. The Father did not create us simply to be objects of His love, but to be channels of His love for Jesus. The Father wants to share His inexpressibly intense and all-consuming love for Jesus with each one of us.

This verse gives us a profound revelation and an awesome promise. It is a revelation because in all creation, only we are designed to be channels of the Father's love for Jesus. The stars may declare God's glory, but they do not flow with His love. We are the only beings who God created in His image to share His awesome love for Jesus.[1]

This verse is also a powerful promise because Jesus has made it His work to fill us with the Father's love. Jesus does not pray futile prayers and here He asks God for a reality He knows can come to pass. If we have the faith, Jesus has both the desire and the power to fill us with the Father's love. He is just waiting to hear the words, *"Let Your will be done."* If we speak those words, the Holy Spirit will begin to pour out the Father's love for Jesus into our hearts to the full extent that our faith allows. And it will feel awesome.[2]

I have made your name known to them

In John 17:26, Jesus promises that He will continue to make the name of the Father known to us. In *First Love,* we learned how Scripture uses a person's name to speak of their character and nature.[3] So the Father's name is not just a word such as Jehovah, Yahweh, Elohim or God. Rather, the Father's name embodies His whole nature of pure love, true holiness, extravagant goodness, infinite grace, and unending compassion.

The term *make known* comes from the Greek word *ginosko,* which we learned means to know, especially through personal experience. From the very beginning of our walk with Jesus, His heart has always been to reveal the Father to us in a personal way. He wants to take us beyond just learning about the Father and enable us to know Him by experiencing His nature of love and goodness for ourselves.

So that the love You have for Me may be in them, and I in them

Beyond bringing us into salvation, Christ's ongoing ministry to us is two-fold. He will continue to make the Father known to us so that:

1. The Father's love for Jesus can flow through us, and
2. Jesus Himself can live in unity with us.

This verse lets us see our design of love from two different angles. From the Father's perspective, we are created to be channels of His love for Jesus. From Jesus' perspective, we are created to live in unity with Him and share His wholehearted love for the Father. When we bring these two aspects of our creation together, we discover that God has made us to live in the middle of the divine flow of love between the Father and the Son. This is why we exist! God is now inviting us to participate in the awesome glory of His love forever.

I in them

The love that flows between the Father and Son through the Spirit unites them as One, which means that it is impossible to separate the presence of Christ from the love of the Father. The Father's love effortlessly draws us deeper into union with Jesus.

As our unity with Jesus grows, we share more of Jesus' love for the Father and our hearts are enlarged for more of the Father's love for Jesus. This brings us into an awesome cascading cycle of love and unity. Love creates unity, which increases our capacity for more love, which then increases our unity with Jesus. And it never needs to end. We can always experience greater depths of God within this beautiful flow of divine love.

This flow of love is the passion and reason behind our design. This is why Jesus came. It was not just about getting us into heaven. The goal of the cross was always to remove the blockage of sin so that the Father's love for Jesus could live in us and we could be one with Christ. This is our inheritance and Jesus has committed Himself to making it a reality. He is simply asking for our permission. Will we say "Yes" to the call of love?

Pray

Jesus, I hear your prayer. Please make the Father's name known to me so that His love for you can live in me and we can be one. Father, please fill me with your love for Jesus and let our love and unity increase!

3 | Unique in Love

1 John 4:19
We love, because He first loved us.

In His grace, God has made every aspect of our design of love possible. Jesus died to set us free from everything within us that opposes love. He was then raised from the dead so that we could live a life of love in unity with Him. In every way it is true: we can only love because He first loved us.

The Father created each one of us to be a unique expression of His love for Jesus. This means that no one can love Jesus in the same way that you can. *No one.* We must refuse to think that other people are more qualified to love Jesus than us or that He would prefer someone else's love over our own. It is simply not true. God has made you different from everyone else for a reason. He has reserved a unique place in His heart for your unique love that no one else can ever fill. Therefore, if you do not come into your design then no one else will be able to make up for the blessing lost to Jesus by your absence. He will lose and you will lose and everyone around you will lose. It is therefore essential that we all personally own and pursue our place in God's flow of love. We must contend for love.

We take our place in this divine flow of love by daily devoting our lives to the first command. The enemy will fight with his full strength to keep us out of love and so we must fight back. At times, the enemy may try to distract us with the pleasures of the world. We must respond by keeping our hearts and vision pure. At other times, he may try to use fear or anxiety and so we must be ready to stand in the faith that God has given us. Sometimes, he may try to convince us that our past failures have disqualified us from the call to love. If this happens, we need to remember two things:

1. No matter what we have done or what we may think, the first and greatest command remains as a constant.[1] At no point in time is anyone ever excused or disqualified from its call. And because God promises to make it possible, everyone can live in the reality of the first command. It is never too difficult, nor is it ever out of reach.

2. The Father's design of love guarantees that He will never give up on us. No matter how badly we have failed or how unworthy we may feel, God is always willing to restore us. Why? Because the Father's ultimate goal is to pour out His love upon Jesus in us and through us. For the Father to abandon us, He would have to abandon a potential channel of His love for Jesus. It is unthinkable that this should ever happen. If we are alive and willing, God will do whatever it takes to restore us to a place where we can share His love for Jesus.

What Profit?

Once we start pursuing our design of love, one of the greatest temptations we face is to start acting in our own strength to do good works for God. Love always flows through our works, but by themselves, our works do not lead us into love. As soon as we start to trust in our works rather than in Jesus' love and presence within us, we step outside God's design for us and quietly fall from grace.

> Job 22:2-3 (NKJV)
> Can a man be profitable to God,
>   though he who is wise may be profitable to himself?
> Is it any pleasure to the Almighty that you are righteous?
> Or is it gain to Him that you make your ways blameless?

Often it can be challenging to accept that the Father has created us to be channels of His love. Many of us have been raised to believe that God created us solely to give Him glory by doing good works and living righteously. But here Eliphaz asks Job an important question: What pleasure or profit does God get from our righteousness?

If we define righteousness as merely doing good works, then the answer is *nothing*. God exists beyond creation and He is already infinite in His glory, immeasurably happy, and entirely complete in Himself. He is more humble than we could ever imagine, and so He does not need us to glorify Him. If all humanity combined all its good works throughout all of history, it would add nothing at all to God.

However, if we define righteousness as living according to our design, our answer to Eliphaz's question changes. What gain does God receive if we are righteous? When we live as channels of love, our righteousness allows more of the Father's love to flow to Jesus. This flow of love is the real profit that God receives through our lives and it is the very reason for our creation.

Nothing but Grace

"Grace means there is nothing I can do to make God love me more, and nothing I can do to make God love me less."

– Phillip Yancey[2]

This a simple but powerful statement that reveals the place of works in our design of love. God's love is not conditional on our works, our obedience, or our affections towards Him. For while we were still sinners, God made the greatest expression of love in all eternity: He gave His only Son for us. We did not earn this love because there are no works that could be worthy of such love. God's love has always been a gift, priceless beyond measure and so always free. Therefore, nothing we can do can make God love us more than He already does right now. All we can do is rest and receive His love.

This truth is a double-edged blade that needs to be handled with great care. On one side it has the power to free us from futile works by showing us that striving to earn God's love is like striving to make the sun rise. It is a pointless waste of time and energy that makes no sense. However, on the other side, resting on the fact that we cannot make God love us any more or less than He already does can open the door to complacency. For if God already loves with an infinite love, then why bother with prayer or good works or worship? If we cannot make Him love us any less, then why not sin?

When we think like this, we fail to understand God's purpose for our lives. God did not create us just to be objects of His love and so we cannot achieve our purpose simply by receiving His love. Our purpose in life is only found as the Father's love for Jesus flows through us. This requires us not just to rest and receive love, but to act and release love. This is where we are empowered. This is why what we do matters because we can always increase our capacity for the love. So while there is nothing we can do to increase God's love *for* us, there is a lot we can do to increase His love *through* us.

Press on to Maturity

Hebrews 6:1a (NASB)

Therefore leaving the elementary teaching about the Christ, let us press on to maturity…

The call to maturity is a call to expand the capacity of our hearts so more of God's love can flow through us. As spiritual infants, we enjoy playing in the shallows of love, where we find all the wonderful emotions of being an object of God's love. We enjoy the shallows because they are safe and incur no cost. Yet our capacity to love God is limited in the shallows. If we are to bring greater love and blessing to God in our lifetime then we need to go deeper. We need to move beyond the emotions of love into the active, selfless, sacrificial love of God. The depths of Love call out to us: *Will you come deeper into love? Will you become more one with Christ? Will you leave your old life behind to find your true life in love?*

This call to maturity is one we must consciously choose. For even though the Father loves Jesus so infinitely, He cannot flow authentic love through us unless we have a genuine choice to participate in His love. This is simply the nature of love. If God forced us to love, He would be enslaving us and He would cease to be love. This of course cannot happen. Love does not force or control others, no matter how good the intentions or how great the consequences. Love always sets people free to choose who they will be.

For this reason, it is important that we make a clear choice to become a living channel of the Father's love for Jesus. This vision calls us to lay down every other goal in life. The world would tell us that the value of our life is only found in what we do. It wants us to find significance outside love and so the world tempts us to focus on developing a ministry or a career or pursuing material wealth. Yet our purpose can never be found in what we do. Our purpose is only found in sharing the Father's love for Jesus and living in unity with Him. There is no higher call and there is no better life. All of this—everything that we call life and creation—it is all about Jesus. It always has been about Him.

Not About Us

"You mean it's not all about us?"

A woman asked the question in a small group study we were doing on our purpose in life. Some people in the group laughed but she was serious. She had been taught her entire Christian life that God did everything because of His great love for us. It therefore required a significant shift in her thinking to believe that God created us not only to receive His love but to flow His love back to Him. This challenged her to rethink her place in creation and the focus of her life. Previously she had been fitting God into her self-oriented life, something she was sure He would be happy to do because of His great love. But now the challenge was to begin fitting her life into God's design, no longer living for herself but for the love of Christ.

We have only a short time on earth so let us be quick to take our place in creation and eternity. The sooner we increase our capacity to share God's love, the more love Jesus will receive from the Father through us. So let us enlarge our hearts and press on to maturity!

Pray

Father, thank you for creating me to share your love for Jesus and to be one with Christ. Please share more of your love and desire for Christ with me.

4 | Value in Love

In the parable of the unforgiving servant, Jesus portrays God as a king who forgives a great debt. Through this parable, Jesus shows us that forgiveness concerns more than sin. It has to do with the value that God invested in our lives and the debt that arose because of that value. Only when we learn why our lives are so valuable to God can we discover why our debt is so great and why the cross is even greater.

Matthew 18:23-35

"Therefore the kingdom of heaven may be compared to a king who wished to settle accounts with his servants. When he began to settle, one was brought to him who owed him ten thousand talents. And since he could not pay, his master ordered him to be sold, with his wife and children and all that he had, and payment to be made. So the servant fell on his knees, imploring him, 'Have patience with me, and I will pay you everything.' And out of pity for him, the master of that servant released him and forgave him the debt. But when that same servant went out, he found one of his fellow servants who owed him a hundred denarii, and seizing him, he began to choke him, saying, 'Pay what you owe.' So his fellow servant fell down and pleaded with him, 'Have patience with me, and I will pay you.' He refused and went and put him in prison until he should pay the debt. When his fellow servants saw what had taken place, they were greatly distressed, and they went and reported to their master all that had taken place. Then his master summoned him and said to him, 'You wicked servant! I forgave you all that debt because you pleaded with me. And should not you have had mercy on your fellow servant, as I had mercy on you?' And in anger his master delivered him to the jailers, until he should pay all his debt. So also my heavenly Father will do to every one of you, if you do not forgive your brother from your heart."

To understand this parable, we need to look at the value of a talent. In Jesus' day, a talent was a weight of gold. The average annual wage for a labourer was 300 silver coins, known as denarii. One talent was worth around 6,000 denarii or about twenty years of work.[1]

The servant had a debt of ten thousand talents—the equivalent of 60 million days' wages. When Jesus told this parable, His listeners would have understood that the servant had been entrusted with unimaginable wealth, only to lose it and find himself completely unable to repay the debt. The servant cried out for mercy and the king forgave the debt. However, the servant then refused to forgive a man who owed him only a hundred denarii—just four months' wages. The king was outraged that his extreme mercy had not produced even the slightest hint of mercy in the servant's heart. He therefore withdrew his forgiveness and reinstated the debt.

Like the servant, we can have people in our lives that we need to forgive. We may have suffered at the hands of others; we may have been abused, betrayed, rejected, neglected, insulted, deceived, slandered, manipulated, robbed or hurt by others. When we are genuinely wounded by someone it can be a struggle to forgive because we tend to see justice as an essential part of our healing. Amid the struggle, we can focus so much on the wrong done to us that we lose sight of the value of our own debt before God. Jesus calls us to refocus our hearts and take on His perspective. The simple message of the parable is that we must forgive others from our heart because no matter what wrong they have done to us, their debt to us will never even begin to approach the debt that we owe to God.

But why do we have a debt with God? And why is our debt so great?

Debt of Love

When we take a loan, we become indebted to the lender. Debt is always created by the transfer of value. Because of the value required for a debt to exist, our debt to God did not start with our sin but with our creation. As created beings, we have been made with a specific purpose *and an obligation to our Creator to fulfil that purpose.* That obligation is our debt.

We can see this in the natural realm. Whatever we invent always has a specific design. Our invention owes its existence to us and it repays its debt by functioning according to its design. For example, in the mountain region of southern New Zealand, there is a system of canals that channel water between three lakes. This water then flows through a series of hydropower stations to create electricity. When these canals were built, the investors did not value the canals by the cost of their construction. Instead, the value of the canals was based on the profit they would bring when they began to flow with water. Apart from the water, the canals are worthless. Yet these canals are worth billions of dollars because of the water that flows through them and the power that water generates. The canals owe their existence to the people that made them, and they repay that debt by channelling the water.

2 Corinthians 4:7
But we have this treasure in jars of clay, to show that the surpassing power belongs to God and not to us.

In many ways we are like the canals—humble jars of clay made to flow with the love of God. And like the canals, from the first moment of our creation, before we had done anything righteous or selfish, we had a debt to our Creator. We owed Him our very existence and the only way we could repay our debt was to live as channels of His love for Jesus.

1 Corinthians 13:2-3
And if I have prophetic powers, and understand all mysteries and all knowledge, and if I have all faith, so as to remove mountains, but have not love, I am nothing. And if I give all my possessions to feed the poor, and if I surrender my body to be burned, but do not have love, it profits me nothing.

As we saw earlier, in the spiritual realm, love is the only substance of eternal value. Even the "good works" that we do— prophesying, moving in spiritual gifts, feeding the poor, or even sacrificing our lives—all our works depend on love to give them value. Without love, we are like canals without water.

However, in the same way that the canals take on the value of the water, we automatically inherit the value of what we let flow through our lives. When we let the love of God flow through us to Jesus, we inherit the value of that love. And the love of the Father for His Son is the most precious element in all eternity. It is a love that is worth far more than any words can possibly describe. We may be worth nothing apart from love, but when the Father's love flows through us, we take on the highest value in all creation.

Settling the Account

Psalm 49:7-9

Truly no man can ransom another,
> or give to God the price of his life,
> for the ransom of their life is costly
> and can never suffice,
> that he should live on forever
> and never see the pit.

So great is the value that God invested in us that Scripture says, "no man can ransom another or give to God the price of his life". There is simply no way we could ever come close to repaying our debt to God.

Only when we see the awesome value that God puts on our lives can we start to appreciate the full cost of our selfishness. When we chose to live for ourselves rather than for God, we shut down a conduit of love between the Father and Jesus. We closed our hearts to God, wasted our inheritance, and denied Jesus a unique measure of the Father's love. This is the real nature and impact of our sin. Sin is not merely "missing the mark" of righteousness; it is failing to live in our design of love. This failure is felt by both the Father and Son more than we could ever imagine.

Through the loss of love, our sin and selfishness incurred a life-debt with God that we could never hope to settle. Every moment that the Father's love flows through a person to Jesus is so eternally precious that we could never hope to redeem even a single wasted moment. No matter how long or short the life, its ransom is simply too costly. It is beyond the reach of every religion and every person.

Legalism would have us try to repay our debt to God through our good works. Yet Jesus expressed the scale of our debt in this parable. If we were to try to work off our debt, we would need more than 60 million days to do good works for God. Nothing we could do could ever earn our forgiveness or redemption from God. Jesus went on to expose the full extent of our debt when He gave His life to cancel out the certificate of debt that stood against us.[2] The Son of Love, the King of kings and Lord of lords, the Mighty God, through whom and for whom all creation was made; this Jesus gave His life to settle our debt with God.[3]

Matthew 5:23-24

"So if you are offering your gift at the altar and there remember that your brother has something against you, leave your gift there before the altar and go. First be reconciled to your brother, and then come and offer your gift."

Only when we understand our design to of love can we see why God values our relationships so much. Here Jesus says that when we bring an offering to God, if we realise that we have a broken relationship with another believer, then we need to stop. There is no point in singing a song of praise to God or offering our money because it will not be acceptable to God. Why? Because Jesus died that we might become one in Him. In John 17, Jesus prays with all His passion for love and unity in His people.[4] So when we tolerate a broken relationship or hold an offence against someone—including our spouse, parents, or children—we act against Christ's prayer in direct opposition to God's will.

The Father wants every relationship we have with other believers to be a channel through which He can love Jesus. But because of offence, we break our unity and deliberately stop the flow of love. This is devastating beyond words to the heart of God. God has given us the highest honour in all creation: to be one with Him as a living expression of His love. And we would despise the honour by tolerating offence? We would deny Jesus a measure of the Father's love through us because of a hurt or injustice? And then we would still pretend to worship Him? This must never happen!

God can work all things for good and He delights to bring forth brilliance out of our brokenness. If we are willing to restore our relationships, He will pour out His love and blessing into them. Many times, we can do this simply by humbling ourselves, talking honestly, listening respectfully, and forgiving one another. But at other times, there may be a struggle. In the face of the struggle, we need to remember that God's design for us depends on our ability to forgive others from our heart. Even though it may seem impossibly difficult, God has promised that He will give us the strength we need to forgive others. We do not need to forgive others for their sake, but for His. As we draw on His strength and choose to forgive those who have hurt us, the Holy Spirit can clear away the blockages of our heart so that our love for Jesus can flow again.

At the cross, Jesus performed the ultimate act of love by sacrificing His life to repay our debt to God. Jesus died and was raised back to life so that we could fulfil our design of love. Now, through His Spirit, Jesus continues to draw us deeper. He calls us: *"Let all those who thirst for love come to me! Let me fill you with more of My Father's love. Call on Me and I will answer you. Seek Me and you will find Me and discover true life in union with Me. Resist no longer, for I created you to be one with Me in eternal love. Come to me!"*

Pray

Father, I thank you for the immense value that you have invested in me. Please help me to see this value in others. Please reach out to others through me so that they might come to know their true worth as well. I repent from all unforgiveness and ask you to help me to truly forgive anyone that has hurt me. Please soften my heart again so that we can fully love people together.

5 | Into our Inheritance

Ephesians 1:3-4

Blessed be the God and Father of our Lord Jesus Christ, who has
blessed us in Christ with every spiritual blessing in the heavenly
places, even as he chose us in him before the foundation of the world,
that we should be holy and blameless before him.

Because of His limitless love, God has given us every single spiritual blessing
in Christ Jesus. But is this really true? And if so, does this mean that every
believer already has *every* spiritual blessing in Christ?

Psalm 105:44

He gave them also the lands of the nations,
    and they took possession of the fruit of the peoples' toil...

The people of Israel were given the Promised Land while they were still in
Egypt. It was their inheritance, but they had to go on a journey before they
could take possession of the land. In the same way, God has given us an
awesome spiritual inheritance in Christ. This means we have ownership of
every spiritual blessing in Christ Jesus and are legally entitled to each one.
However, though we receive this inheritance when we first believe, we do not
experience all these blessings in a single moment of time. Instead, like Israel,
we need to go on a journey to possess our inheritance.

To possess something means that we personally experience it in our lives.
Inheritance is the theory; possession is the reality—our actual experience. In
the natural realm, though we may inherit great wealth, if we fail to take
possession of that wealth then it is of no real value to us. So while God has
given us an inheritance that surpasses all imagination, for it to be of any value
to us, we need to take hold of it and let it change our lives. We need to go
from theory to reality.

Into Reality

John 8:32

"...and you will know the truth, and the truth will set you free."

The word translated as *know* in this verse is the Greek word *ginosko,* which means "to know, especially through personal experience."[1] In terms of everyday facts, ginosko can refer to intellectual knowledge, but in the context of spiritual growth, ginosko speaks of the knowledge of the heart. It is the deep, inner knowledge that begins with revelation and is completed in experience.

The word translated here as *truth* is the Greek word *aletheia,* which means "truth, what is true to fact; reality."[2] With a deeper appreciation of both *aletheia* and *ginosko,* John 8:32 could be amplified to read:

"...and you will personally experience the reality of the truth, and that reality will set you free."

This verse applies to every blessing that is ours in Christ—all the love, joy, peace, faith and glory that is available as our inheritance. For example, as we personally experience the love of God, His love sets us free from our fear and selfishness. When we experience the reality of peace, we are set free from our stress and anxiety. As we come into our inheritance in joy, we find freedom from grief and depression. And so it continues. Freedom comes through experience.

All these blessings are stored up for us as an inheritance just waiting to be experienced. So how can we access our inheritance in Christ?

John 16:13

"When the Spirit of truth comes, he will guide you into all the truth [reality], for he will not speak on his own authority, but whatever he hears he will speak, and he will declare to you the things that are to come."

God has given us His Spirit to lead us into all reality. He sees what we need at each stage of our journey and tells us about the things to come. When the Holy Spirit speaks to us, His voice sets in motion a process that leads us from revelation to the reality of that word.[3] For some aspects of our inheritance, revelation and reality may come on the same day. For others, the process may span many years.

Revelation

John 17:17

"Sanctify them in the truth; your word is truth."

The word of God is truth; it reveals the reality of our inheritance in Christ. However, the call of Scripture is not that we would merely know the truth, but that we would *experience* the truth. For example, the Bible does not speak of God's forgiveness just so we can build an understanding or theology of forgiveness. The Scriptures speak of forgiveness to inspire us to turn to God and actually experience His forgiveness. This is not something that we can do ourselves. Even repentance only happens with the help of the Holy Spirit.[4]

If we read the Scriptures without leaning on the Holy Spirit, we might accept the forgiveness of God on an intellectual level and yet still live with a sense of guilt and shame over our sin. We need to remember that only the Holy Spirit can make the truth real for us. So when we read about forgiveness, we need to ask for a revelation of what it means for God to forgive us and to forget our sin *forever*. When He shows us how God's forgiveness completely restores our innocence before Him; when He makes it real for us on a heart-level, we will then feel the joy of having a truly clear conscience before God.

This work of revelation can be seen in the story of Jesus meeting with two of His disciples on the road to Emmaus.[5] Jesus hid His identity from them and as they walked, He shared revelations from the Scriptures and opened their eyes to see the truth. Afterwards the disciples said to each other "Didn't our hearts burn within us while he talked to us on the road, while he opened the Scriptures to us?"

When the Spirit of Jesus opens the Scriptures and brings revelation to us, we too can experience a fire within our hearts that gets ignited by His voice. This fire is the sense of life and excitement that comes with revelation. However, revelation is simply the first step to reality. To experience a truth or receive a new blessing from God, we need to connect revelation to faith, faith to grace, and grace to action.

Faith

> **Romans 10:10, 17**
>
> For with the heart one believes and is justified, and with the mouth one confesses and is saved...So faith comes from hearing, and hearing through the word of Christ.

Scripture says it is "with the heart that one believes" rather than the mind. Faith is not simply an intellectual belief. On the contrary, faith is the confidence of the heart that comes from hearing God speak.[6] Because faith starts with God's voice, Scripture describes faith as both a gift and a fruit of the Spirit.[7] This means that we do not have to try to generate our own faith; we simply need to invite the Holy Spirit to speak to us and bring a revelation to our hearts.

Faith is a gift, but we have a part to play in receiving the gift. One day as I was praying, I felt the Father speak to me about how I had been mishandling the precious gift of faith.

"When I speak into your life, I give you the gift of faith. Yet like so many people, you take the gift, thank Me, and then put the gift on your gift-shelf. The gift sits there, fully wrapped in glistening foil, but never opened and never truly received."

It is important that we learn how to respond to God's voice in a way that allows faith to fill our hearts. So when we hear God speak to us, we need to take some time to unwrap and open the gift. We do this by engaging our imagination and meditating on His truth. Imagination is a bridge between the heart and the mind, and it gives space for the Holy Spirit to make His truth real for us. For example, if God speaks to us about humility, we can unwrap the gift by imagining Jesus taking away our pride and exchanging it with His life-giving humility. We can imagine what it feels like to share His humility, sensing the incredible strength it brings to our soul. As soon as we let the Holy Spirit inspire our imagination, our faith turns into vision and leads us to think and act differently. [8]

Grace

Romans 5:2
Through him we have also obtained access by faith into this grace in which we stand, and we rejoice in hope of the glory of God.

Grace recognises that for a gift to be a gift, it must be unearned and free from any hint of manipulation. If someone gives us a gift only in response to something we have done, then it is not really a gift—it is a payment for our actions. Or if a person gives us a gift to influence us in their favour, then the gift is not a gift—it is a bribe. This principle is also true for our relationship with God. Every blessing God gives us is a gift of His grace. But to ensure that it remains a gift, God cannot release a single blessing to us until we are willing to receive it on His terms: by faith alone.

Faith enables us to receive from God because it compels us to put our confidence in God's *infinite* goodness. He gives us good gifts because God is better and more loving than we could ever dream. In faith, we honour the goodness of the Giver by receiving His gifts without trying to earn them. In faith, we no longer beg God for His blessings, but instead, we thank Him for already giving us an inheritance beyond all imagination. This is the kind of faith that accesses grace, and it is the only way of ensuring that every gift remains a blessing of God's extravagant love and nothing less.

Philippians 2:13
...for it is God who works in you, both to will and to work for his good pleasure.

Faith is conceived by the voice of God, nurtured through Spirit-inspired imagination, and then born into the world through action. Our faith enables us to receive God's grace, which energises us to will *and* to act for His good pleasure. When we act on a revelation, the truth of God then becomes our reality.

Reality

> John 1:17
> For the law was given through Moses; grace and truth [reality] came through Jesus Christ.

The process from revelation to reality begins and ends with Jesus. He gives us His Spirit to bring us revelation and make His truth real for us. As the Spirit of Jesus speaks to us, He creates faith in our hearts, which gives us access to His grace. This grace energises us to act on His truth and experience the awesome reality of each blessing God gives us.

Therefore, if the Spirit of God speaks to you or brings some words of Scripture to life, then recognise that Jesus is speaking *in order to bring you into reality.*[9] Honour God's voice by taking some time to meditate on what the Spirit is saying. Unwrap the gift. Let the Spirit inspire your imagination and bring revelation and faith into your heart. As the confidence of faith is formed within you, it will compel you to take hold of God's grace and put that revelation into action. God's truth will become your reality, and the truth shall set you free.

Pray

Father, thank you for giving me every spiritual blessing in Christ. Thank you for wanting me to live in the reality of all these blessings of my Promised Land. Please help me to become truly confident in your infinite goodness. Help me to hear your voice more clearly and to grow in faith with you. Let us take the next step on this journey together.

6 | You Alone

Titus 3:4-6

But when the goodness and loving kindness of God our Saviour appeared, he saved us, not because of works done by us in righteousness, but according to his own mercy, by the washing of regeneration and renewal of the Holy Spirit, whom he poured out on us richly through Jesus Christ our Saviour.

God is not simply good, He is *goodness.* If we take our concept of goodness and stretch it to the extremes of our imagination, even then, we would not grasp the full extent of God's goodness. God is perfectly, infinitely good. If He was anything less, He would not be God.[1]

Psalm 16:5-6 (NLT)

LORD, you alone are my inheritance, my cup of blessing.
You guard all that is mine.
The land you have given me is a pleasant land.
What a wonderful inheritance!

Goodness is always expressed in giving. Because God's nature is one of unlimited goodness, He must give without any limit and offer us everything He can as gift of His love. And He does exactly that. For in this passage, we find that not only did the Father give us His Son and every single blessing in Christ Jesus, but He also gave us the ultimate gift: *Himself!*[2] The Lord God is our inheritance, and if we have Him, we have everything.

In the last chapter, we saw that while we receive every spiritual blessing in Christ, it takes time to experience these different blessings in our lives. It is the same for our inheritance in God. There are so many different dimensions of relationship we can have with Him, and each one takes time to experience. We can come to know God as our Lord, Saviour, King, Father, Mother, Brother, Teacher, Provider, Judge, Protector, Counsellor, Healer, Comforter, Shepherd, Master, Friend, Helper, and many more.[3] Each of these relationships reveals a different colour of God's love that changes us in a different way.

Jesus as a Friend

All relationships are two-way, living connections that grow with time and mutual investment. There is always a process to building relationships, and every relationship that we can have with God requires something of us. For example, it is every believer's inheritance to know Jesus as a friend. Those who experience this relationship find that Jesus is the ultimate friend. He is always there for us. We can share anything with Him and as our friend, Jesus never condemns us. He always seeks our best, calls us higher, and loves us enough to speak the truth. As a friend, Jesus enjoys just spending time with us and sharing His heart with us.

Sadly, many believers do not personally experience the friendship of Christ. Many of us enjoy relating to Jesus as our saviour and receiving the blessings of His forgiveness, and yet hesitate when He offers His friendship. But why would anyone refuse the gift of friendship with Jesus?

> **John 15:12-15**
> "This is my commandment, that you love one another as I have loved you. Greater love has no one than this, that someone lay down his life for his friends. You are my friends if you do what I command you. No longer do I call you servants, for the servant does not know what his master is doing; but I have called you friends, for all that I have heard from my Father I have made known to you."

Because relationships involve our participation, it is natural for us to focus on those relationships that feel safe and require little of us. Some of us avoid getting to know Jesus as a friend because it involves a higher level of intimacy, self-sacrifice and obedience than it does to know Him as our saviour.[4] Others avoid it because knowing Jesus as our friend requires us to become a friend to Him. This may be challenging for people who have been raised to only relate to Jesus as a master or king. For if we are to relate to Jesus as a friend, we need to let go of all our religious formalities and learn to talk to Jesus honestly from our heart. We need to learn to be comfortable being casual, real, and even emotional with Jesus, knowing that nothing can ever shake His love for us.

While this may seem hard at first, our barriers to friendship are no problem for God. He has given us His Spirit to lead us step by step on our journey into love. And the Spirit wants to help us get to know Jesus as our friend. He simply waits until we are willing.

Knowing the Father

In *First Love*, I shared how God brought me to know Jesus as my provider. The Holy Spirit led me to spend some time meditating on Psalm 23:1, imagining Jesus as my shepherd who would supply all my needs. As I meditated on the word, the Spirit burned His promise of provision into my heart. Ever since then, He has provided everything I have ever needed and more. However, at that early stage in my journey, even though I knew God as my provider, I was still far from knowing Him as my Father. Though I called Him *Father* and could quote many verses about love, my heart was unable to receive the Father's love. It simply was not real for me.

In the parable of the prodigal son, Jesus reveals what is required of us if we are going to get to know God as our Father. Through the two sons, we learn that the only way to know God as our Father is to stop striving for His acceptance and simply surrender to His love. For me, this proved far more difficult than it sounds. My instinct to earn approval was fierce. It took me a long time to realise that as long as I kept striving to earn God's love and affection, I could *never* experience Him as my Father. Why? Because the Father's love and affection are gifts that can never be earned. They are simply not for sale. Because of the priceless nature of the Father's love, there exists an unbreakable spiritual law: good works flow from love, *never to it*.

It was a law I tried to break every day. I truly wanted to please God, so I would constantly try to be a good Christian. I hoped the things I did would inspire God to share His love with me. But even though the Father longed for me to know His love, my striving prevented Him from sharing His love with me. As a result, the two of us missed out on the intimacy that we were both so desperately seeking.[5] I only started getting to know God as my Father when I stopped trying to earn His love.

This highlights the difference between inheritance and possession in our relationship with God. God is our Father and we are all His children, so we all have an inheritance in relating to Him as our Father. But the theory of inheritance is entirely different from the reality of possession. As spiritual infants, we can call God our Father without actually experiencing Him as our infinitely loving, generous, merciful, gracious and affectionate Father. If we want to truly know God as our Father, then we need to die to our own efforts and accept that our Father loves us. He truly, deeply, passionately loves us.

Jesus as our Bridegroom

There are people who teach that because Jesus came to restore us to the Father, once we know God as our Father, the work of Jesus is done and we no longer need to relate to the Son. However, if we stop at knowing God as our Father, then we miss the reason for our creation. The Father created us *for* Jesus. To be sure, God wants us to know Him as our Father, but He also wants us to share His love for Jesus and see us become one with Christ. This is His ultimate goal.

Every relationship we can have with God contributes to this goal in a unique way. The love we find in our friendship with Jesus changes us in a different way to the love we receive from the Father. And the unity we share as children of God is different to the unity we experience as His servants.

In our natural lives, the greatest level of love and unity is reserved for marriage. This is also true spiritually. Because the Father wants us to experience the greatest possible love and unity with Jesus, He calls us to know Jesus as our bridegroom.

John 1:29

The next day he saw Jesus coming toward him, and said, "Behold, the Lamb of God, who takes away the sin of the world!"

John 3:28-29

"You yourselves bear me witness, that I said, 'I am not the Christ, but I have been sent before him.' The one who has the bride is the bridegroom. The friend of the bridegroom, who stands and hears him, rejoices greatly at the bridegroom's voice. Therefore this joy of mine is now complete."

John the Baptist spoke of Jesus coming in two key roles: The lamb of God who takes away the sin of the world, and the bridegroom who has the bride. Jesus comes as the first to enable the second. He is the lamb of God who takes away our sin *so that* He can become one with us in covenant love. Love is the goal of salvation.

Ephesians 5:25-32

Husbands, love your wives, as Christ loved the church and gave himself up for her, that he might sanctify her, having cleansed her by the washing of water with the word, so that he might present the church to himself in splendour, without spot or wrinkle or any such thing, that she might be holy and without blemish. In the same way husbands should love their wives as their own bodies. He who loves his wife loves himself. For no one ever hated his own flesh, but nourishes and cherishes it, just as Christ does the church, because we are members of his body. "Therefore a man shall leave his father and mother and hold fast to his wife, and the two shall become one flesh." This mystery is profound, and I am saying that it refers to Christ and the church.

Isaiah 54:5

For your Maker is your husband,
the LORD of hosts is his name;
and the Holy One of Israel is your Redeemer,
the God of the whole earth he is called.

Scripture speaks of knowing God in a relational way because God is relational. He calls Himself our Father because like the perfect father, God is loving, encouraging, nurturing, uncompromising, empowering, strong, and tender. He is not afraid to correct and discipline us, and He never gives up on us. As our heavenly Father, God is only ever good to us and His heart is always to see us grow to maturity.

In the same way, Scripture speaks of Jesus as a husband, because like the perfect husband, Jesus loves us, cherishes us, and delights in us. He protects and empowers us. He lavishes us with His extreme goodness and brings out the very best in us. He talks with us and shares the affections of His heart and soul with us. He faithfully leads us and provides for us in all humility, purity and adoring love.

It is important to note that knowing Jesus as our husband has nothing to do with our sexuality at all. Just as God does not intend for women to feel like they need to become masculine to know the blessings of being a "son of God," neither does He want men to think that we need to become feminine in any way to become the bride of Christ.[6] It is simply used as a metaphor because marriage represents the highest level of love, devotion and intimacy available in our human relationships.

Because knowing Jesus as our husband is about coming into a new realm of unity with Jesus, it is no threat to masculinity. In fact, the qualities that we would think of as masculine such as honour, strength, courage, loyalty, the instinct to protect and provide, the desire to equip others and so on; all these qualities find their source and perfection in Jesus. Therefore, knowing Jesus as our husband brings men into a unity that enhances rather than reduces masculinity. Through this relationship, Jesus perfects the strength of men by taking us on a journey into dependency. He increases our sense of honour by sharing His humility with us. He uses intimacy to add to our integrity. He perfects our power by making us dependent on Him. And He affirms our sense of loyalty by calling us into the covenant of the bride—a commitment to a new life with Him. In every way, becoming the bride of Christ empowers men to be truly men.

Likewise, women find the qualities of their own unique personalities all enhanced in union with Jesus. He completes the femininity of women and the masculinity of men, and He does it through a spiritual marriage. As we become one with Christ, we become more ourselves than ever before.

Pray

Father, please show me which relationship you would like to take me into next and how I can participate. Please remove every fear and every barrier that keeps me from knowing you.

7 | A Time for Love

Scripture presents Jesus both as a bridegroom and a husband because there is a journey into every marriage. As it is in the natural realm, we begin with a friendship before moving to engagement and then into union. We can think of it like growing from infancy to maturity in our relationship with Jesus. The more we grow in Christ, the more our love matures until the romance begins and we encounter Jesus as our bridegroom—the lover of our soul! Once we possess the bridegroom relationship, we can then come into union with Him and know Him as our husband.

This process of relationship can be seen in the following passage:

Ezekiel 16:1-14 (NKJV)
Again the word of the LORD came to me, saying, "Son of man, cause Jerusalem to know her abominations, and say, 'Thus says the LORD God to Jerusalem: "Your birth and your nativity are from the land of Canaan; your father was an Amorite and your mother a Hittite. As for your nativity, on the day you were born your navel cord was not cut, nor were you washed in water to cleanse you; you were not rubbed with salt nor wrapped in swaddling cloths. No eye pitied you, to do any of these things for you, to have compassion on you; but you were thrown out into the open field, when you yourself were loathed on the day you were born.

"And when I passed by you and saw you struggling in your own blood, I said to you in your blood, 'Live!' Yes, I said to you in your blood, 'Live!' I made you thrive like a plant in the field; and you grew, matured, and became very beautiful. Your breasts were formed, your hair grew, but you were naked and bare.

"When I passed by you again and looked upon you, indeed your time was the time of love; so I spread My wing over you and covered your nakedness. Yes, I swore an oath to you and entered into a covenant with you, and you became Mine," says the LORD God.

"Then I washed you in water; yes, I thoroughly washed off your blood, and I anointed you with oil. I clothed you in embroidered cloth and gave you sandals of badger skin; I clothed you with fine linen and covered you with silk. I adorned you with ornaments, put bracelets on your wrists, and a chain on your neck. And I put a jewel in your nose, earrings in your ears, and a beautiful crown on your head. Thus you were adorned with gold and silver, and your clothing was of fine linen, silk, and embroidered cloth. You ate pastry of fine flour, honey, and oil. You were exceedingly beautiful, and succeeded to royalty. Your fame went out among the nations because of your beauty, for it was perfect through My splendour which I had bestowed on you," says the LORD God.

Here God speaks of the maturing of His people. Jerusalem was born in iniquity, continuing in the selfishness and sin of her ancestors. She was cast out into the open field and left to die.

But God saw her and chose her. He had compassion on her and spoke the words that brought her to life. God washed her and cared for her. She matured and grew and became beautiful. Then she came into her time of love. God spread His wing over her and made a covenant with her, and she became His. He then made her even more beautiful than before, exceedingly beautiful, and He elevated her to royalty. The glory of her beauty became known throughout the world, for it was perfect through His splendour.

Romans 15:4
For whatever was written in former days was written for our instruction, that through endurance and through the encouragement of the Scriptures we might have hope.

The things that happened to Israel were written down for our instruction. The passage in Ezekiel was written not only as an account of Israel's history but as a picture of our own spiritual growth in Christ. It speaks of our journey from being born again to our entrance into a realm of glorious love: that of becoming the bride of Christ.

Dead in Sin

Ephesians 2:1-3

And you were dead in the trespasses and sins in which you once walked, following the course of this world, following the prince of the power of the air, the spirit that is now at work in the sons of disobedience— among whom we all once lived in the passions of our flesh, carrying out the desires of the body and the mind, and were by nature children of wrath, like the rest of mankind.

Like the baby that was left to die, apart from Christ we were helpless. Though we were physically alive, we were spiritually dead in our selfishness.[1] Yet as He did for Israel, God saw us in our hopelessness and spoke to us: *Live!* God's word was spirit and life to us, infused with the power of salvation. Like a baby waiting to die, there was nothing we could do to save ourselves. But by His grace and love, God looked upon us and brought us out of death and into life.

Born Again

When we first come to faith in Jesus, we are born again as spiritual babes with a lifetime of growth in front of us. Every newborn baby is born with a limited capacity to relate to others or to give love. Babies simply receive. They crave provision, comfort and affection. In our newborn state, God comes to us as El Shaddai.[2] He loves us and nourishes us with the milk of His word, giving us all the nurture and affection we need to live and grow.[3] As our Father, God knows that in our infancy we are more like containers of love than channels of love. But God is patient. He knows that if we continue to mature, our time of love will come.

You grew, matured and became very beautiful

Part of maturing is actively turning away from those things that keep us in infancy. Pride keeps us in infancy by making us unteachable. Isolation prevents us from maturing through relationships. Complacency stops us from growing by removing our desire for change. Mediators keep us in infancy by speaking for God instead of teaching us how to hear God's voice for ourselves. Worldly pleasures keep us in spiritual infancy by distracting us away from the journey of love. Our call is to turn away from such things and press on to maturity.

Your breasts were formed

1 Thessalonians 5:8
But since we belong to the day, let us be sober, having put on the breastplate of faith and love, and for a helmet the hope of salvation.

The breastplate of righteousness is also called the breastplate of faith and love. As Israel grew up, her breasts were formed. In a spiritual sense, the development of the breasts speaks of growing in faith and love.

"Faith is the beginning, love the end. And these two in union are divine." – Ignatius

It is for good reason that Scripture says that we are "saved by grace through faith" and that "we have gained access by faith into the grace in which we now stand."[4] Grace cannot be earned—it is a gift that can only be received through faith. Faith is therefore the first step to love, for love itself is a gift of grace.

Romans 10:17
So faith comes from hearing, and hearing through the [spoken] word of Christ.

Faith comes from hearing the voice of God. If we want to grow in faith, then we need to start by learning to listen. Infants take time to listen to the sound of their parents' voice and learn their language. It is the same for us. The more we listen and learn to discern our Father's voice, the more faith we receive from Him. As our faith grows, His grace empowers us to love more. When we act in love, our faith is made complete. Like the breasts of the bride, our faith and love grow together in union, bringing us to a place of spiritual maturity.

Your time was the time of love; so I spread My wing over you
Ruth 3:9
He said, "Who are you?" And she answered, "I am Ruth, your servant. Spread your wings over your servant, for you are a redeemer."

In Scripture, coming under the wing is a metaphor for getting married.[5] When Ruth said to Boaz: "Take your maidservant under your wings," Boaz understood that Ruth was proposing marriage. Boaz is a type of Christ. Just as Boaz was a redeemer and husband to Ruth, so Jesus is our redeemer and our husband.

When God spreads His wing over His people in Ezekiel 16, He takes them as His wife and becomes their divine husband. In terms of our journey, when we reach the time of love, Jesus does the same for us. He spreads His wing over us, covers us, and becomes our security, refuge, love and joy.

I swore an oath to you and entered into a covenant with you
The marriage relationship is created through a mutual covenant—an absolute, lifelong commitment to love. Just as there are many depths to salvation to explore and grow in, there are also many depths to being in covenant with God. The covenant of marriage is one of those depths.

We enter the marriage covenant by devoting our entire lives—all we are and all we have—to loving Jesus and living in unity with Him. The commitment that Jesus makes to us is similar. Jesus promises to be faithful to love us with an unending, unbreakable love. He commits Himself to taking us ever deeper into His love and to living in unity with us. Beyond this, Jesus also commits Himself to keeping our side of the covenant as well! By circumcising our hearts and filling us with the Father's love, Jesus enables us to love Him with all our heart and soul. He has made the promise and He has the power to keep His covenant and to help us to keep ours. If we will trust Him, He will do it.

And you became Mine

Song of Songs 6:3a
"I am my beloved's and my beloved is mine."

The marriage relationship is one of mutual possession: we are God's and He is ours. He is our first love, our life, our reason, and our passion. We are His beloved, His delight, and His perfect one.

The marriage relationship calls us to be wholly possessed by Christ. This means that we need to contend for love by declaring war on anything that would try to divide our heart or steal our affections. Our one focus in life is to love Jesus with everything we are and have.

I adorned you with gold and silver

In the marriage relationship, God lavishes spiritual wealth upon us. He makes us even more beautiful with the gold of His nature and the silver of His redeeming power. Through His Spirit, He adorns us with His character, clothing us in His righteousness, wrapping us in humility, and crowning us with glory.

You were exceedingly beautiful, and succeeded to royalty

The heart of the Father is to prepare an exceedingly beautiful bride for His Son. When we are ready, the Father presents us to Jesus, who takes us in marriage, and we succeed to royalty. This brings us into a new realm of authority and power. Our authority flows directly from our unity with Jesus and it releases the power of His love on earth. It is not an authority that seeks to dominate the world, but to love the world. This is the true authority that Jesus wants to rule and reign through, and it is an authority that is only found through marriage love and union.

Your fame went out among the nations because of your beauty, for it was perfect through My splendour which I bestowed upon you
God's desire is that the world would be in awe of our beauty. He wants His love to shine through us with such brilliance that people are left stunned and undone. Only then will the words of Christ be found true and we will become known in the world by our love for one another. People will see our love and be drawn to its Source. In all of this, we will remain humble, knowing that our beauty is entirely from God. He makes our beauty perfect through His splendour which He lavishes upon us, and it is all for His great glory!

Pray
Father, thank you for bringing me to life. Thank you for nurturing me. I want to become a glorious and beautiful gift for your Son. Please show me how I can come into my time of love.

8 | Covenant of Love

Genesis 24:67

Then Isaac brought her into the tent of Sarah his mother and took Rebekah, and she became his wife, and he loved her.

When Abraham sent his servant to find a bride for his son, God led the servant to Rebekah. Rebekah's family blessed her to go and devote her life to the man that God had prepared her for. When she arrived in the new land, she met Isaac. They lay together and she became his wife.

When Isaac and Rebekah were married there was no wedding ceremony, instead, there was only a commitment followed by a union. As the centuries passed, the Hebrew culture developed, and formal betrothals and wedding ceremonies became a traditional part of a Jewish marriage. Yet even with these changes, at the core of marriage there remained just two essential elements: covenant and union.

Because God created the marriage relationship, He honours these two elements in our marriage to Jesus. In this chapter we look at the covenant of marriage.

Betrothed Forever

Hosea 2:14-20

"Therefore, behold, I will allure her,
 and bring her into the wilderness,
 and speak tenderly to her.
And there I will give her her vineyards
 and make the Valley of Achor a door of hope.
And there she shall answer as in the days of her youth,
 as at the time when she came out of the land of Egypt.

"And in that day, declares the LORD, you will call me 'My Husband,' and no longer will you call me 'My Baal.' For I will remove the names of the Baals from her mouth, and they shall be remembered by name no more. And I will make for them a covenant on that day with the beasts of the field, the birds of the heavens, and the creeping things of the ground. And I will abolish the bow, the sword, and war from the land, and I will make you lie down in safety. And I will betroth you to me forever. I will betroth you to me in righteousness and in justice, in steadfast [covenant] love and in mercy. I will betroth you to me in faithfulness. And you shall know the LORD."

In this passage, God revealed His heart towards Israel and His desire to allure her out of her idolatry and into intimate, covenant love. He did not want to be a master (baal) to Israel and to possess her as an obedient servant. Rather, He wanted to be a husband who could enjoy the love, devotion and affection of His people. To this end, God betrothed His people to Himself in covenant love.

Song of Solomon: 8:5a
Who is that coming up from the wilderness,
leaning on her beloved?

Jeremiah 2:2
Thus says the LORD, "I remember the devotion of your youth, your love as a bride, how you followed me in the wilderness, in a land not sown."

The whole of Israel's history is an epic love story. After freeing His people from Egypt, God took Israel into the wilderness and called her to choose a life of love, intimacy and unity with Him. Because love is an unconditional, free gift, God could not force this kind of life upon Israel. Instead, He had to allure His people, inspiring them with the glory of covenant love, while also revealing the futility of a life outside His design. When we read Exodus and Deuteronomy through the lens of love, we can see God spiritually courting His people and preparing His bride.

Exodus 19:5

"Now therefore, if you will indeed obey my voice and keep my covenant, you shall be my treasured possession among all peoples, for all the earth is mine…"

Deuteronomy 7:6

"For you are a people holy to the LORD your God. The LORD your God has chosen you to be a people for his treasured possession, out of all the peoples who are on the face of the earth."

The term *treasured possession* is a deeply affectionate term with romantic overtones more appropriate to the whispers of lovers than the writings of the Law. It is like hearing God say, *"Out of all the people on the earth, I have chosen you. You are my priceless treasure, the jewel of my heart. I have set all my love and affection upon you, so that all the nations might be drawn to me through you. You are just so precious to me. I treasure you my love."*

Chuppah

When Moses ascended Mount Sinai, God covered the top of the mountain with His glory and gave Moses the Law. This exchange on Sinai was like a wedding between God and His people. The covering of glory was like the covering or *chuppah*. The chuppah is a canopy under which the bride and groom come together, and it is still used in Jewish weddings today. It speaks of the presence and covering of God over the marriage.

Ketubah

In addition to the chuppah, Jewish marriages require the signing of a ketubah as part of the covenant process. The ketubah is a legal document that outlines the responsibilities of the husband and wife in marriage and provides a framework of love.

In the wilderness, God gave Moses the Law as His ketubah. The Mosaic Law was a framework of love built around a single command: to love God with all our heart and soul.[1] God's ketubah with Israel guaranteed the blessings that Israel would experience in union with God and outlined Israel's responsibility to be faithful to Him.

Betrothed to One Husband

The heart of God has not changed. Jesus did not die to make us obedient slaves, and He has no desire at all to be a master that rules over us from a distant throne. Jesus wants to be our Husband. The Father created us for loving Jesus, and therefore just as He did for Israel, so God betroths each one of us to His Son.

> **2 Corinthians 11:1-3**
> I wish you would bear with me in a little foolishness. Do bear with me! For I feel a divine jealousy for you, since I betrothed you to one husband, to present you as a pure virgin to Christ. But I am afraid that as the serpent deceived Eve by his cunning, your thoughts will be led astray from a sincere and pure devotion to Christ.

Betrothal is the first stage of marriage. It is an exclusive covenant between a bride and groom that commits them to a future union in marriage.[2] Through Paul, God betrothed the believers at Corinth to one husband: Jesus Christ. However, because God does not force His love upon people, the believers at Corinth were free to go astray. So Paul called them to repent and return to their first love. Like Moses before him, Paul could see God's vision for love, but he struggled to get the people to see past their veils of selfishness and legalism. Like Israel before them, the hearts of God's people were divided.

The Father brought Israel into the wilderness, a dry place free from distraction, to experience His love and enter into a divine romance. Like Israel, we come into our time of love in the wilderness. In the dry places we learn to depend on the goodness and faithfulness of God. God speaks to us and shares His deep desire for intimacy and oneness. He draws us with cords of kindness, enticing us to say "yes" to His love.

Covenant Love

Every marriage is based on a two-way covenant. The nation of Israel had the Law as their ketubah. In the same way, before we can know Jesus as our bridegroom, we need to commit to keeping the terms of our marriage covenant. This commitment is different from the covenant that we entered into when we first received Jesus as our Saviour and were born into the family of God. At that time, we had nothing to offer God but our sin and selfishness. In His grace, God required nothing of us, except that we believe in Jesus Christ and receive His free gift of forgiveness. But now, having matured and come to our time of love, we are called into a new depth of covenant. The marriage covenant is still a covenant of grace, but it is not one-sided. Just as it is in the natural realm, so our marriage covenant with Jesus requires our consent and our active participation. God will not force us into covenant. We must freely agree to the terms of our marriage and then focus on living by those terms. So let us take a look at the fine print of becoming the bride of Christ.

> Mark 12:28-31
>
> And one of the scribes came up and heard them disputing with one another, and seeing that he answered them well, asked him, "Which commandment is the most important of all?" Jesus answered, "The most important is, 'Hear, O Israel: The Lord our God, the Lord is one. And you shall love the Lord your God with all your heart and with all your soul and with all your mind and with all your strength.' The second is this: 'You shall love your neighbour as yourself.' There is no other commandment greater than these."

This passage contains the terms of our covenant with Jesus. If we are to know Jesus as our bridegroom, we must agree to loving Jesus with all our heart, soul, mind, and strength. This is only possible through our union with Jesus and so we must likewise commit ourselves to becoming one with Christ, inviting His emotions, thoughts, and presence to fill our lives. We need to accept that we were bought with a price and we are no longer our own. Jesus now owns everything we are and have—our heart, soul, mind, body, time, wealth, and possessions—and He can now use them all to express His love. As His bride, we agree to obey His voice and to love others, just as He commanded.

This is no small commitment. It is a life-long, irrevocable decision to love Jesus wholeheartedly and to be one with Him. This decision gives God our full permission to remove every obstacle that prevents us from receiving His love or entering into a marriage covenant with Him.

If we are honest, we may find that making this level of commitment to Jesus is beyond us. I remember wanting to commit my whole heart to God but realising that there were parts of my heart that I simply could not give. My heart was too divided; no matter what I decided in my mind, I could not convince my heart to abandon its affections for the world. But God is good. He honours our honesty and will give us the grace we need. For me, I simply prayed, "*Father, I surrender my whole heart to loving Jesus. And those parts of my heart that I cannot give, I ask you to take anyway. Do whatever it takes to possess all of me for your love.*"

If you do not feel completely ready or willing to make this covenant, then step back and ask, "*Am I willing to be willing?*" If so, make that your prayer: "*Lord I am willing to be willing to love you with all my heart and soul. Please give me the hunger I need to make this covenant with you.*"

Deuteronomy 30:6
And the LORD your God will circumcise your heart and the heart of your offspring, so that you will love the LORD your God with all your heart and with all your soul, that you may live.

God does not expect us to commit to or obey the first command in our own strength. He knows it is impossible for us, but He can easily do it. He is the one who spreads His wing over us; He is the one who makes covenant with us and takes us as His own. He is the one who cuts away the selfishness from our hearts and fills us with His love for Jesus. It is all His work, but it only happens with our permission. Our part in this covenant is to agree to love

Him, to obey His voice, and to be one with Him. If we agree to this, He guarantees to make it a reality. This is the inheritance of every believer. This is the life of love that God has prepared for you. This is your call.

Pray

Father, thank you for betrothing me as a bride to your Son. I hear the call to make a covenant of love with Jesus. Please help me to make this covenant and to devote my whole life to loving Jesus.

9 | One with Christ

Betrothal is an agreement that binds us in marriage to Jesus and creates a platform for intimate love and union with Him. In the natural realm, God's design is that sexual union is only holy within the realms of covenant. If we have union within covenant, we are married. If we have sexual union without covenant, we are adulterers, fornicators, or prostitutes. Why? It is because sex is an act of selfless love that is designed to build unity between a husband and wife. The marriage covenant makes this possible by removing the threat of rejection which creates a safe environment for a deep emotional bond to be forged. Simply put, the marriage covenant allows us to give ourselves fully to our spouse knowing that they have given themselves fully to us.

If we engage in sex without a covenant, we prostitute ourselves to each other's lusts and have only a selfish pretence of love. Lust is insatiable and constantly seeks novelty, and so without a covenant, the threat of rejection is often realised, bringing with it great spiritual and emotional damage. For this reason, Scripture calls us to keep ourselves pure for marriage.

This principle of covenant is true both in the natural and the spiritual. As a bridegroom, Jesus reserves a realm of intimate knowledge for those who would enter a covenant of love with Him. This does not mean that God favours some believers over others. Every believer has been given the same inheritance in Christ, and we are all called to keep the first command and to become one with Jesus. But do we all answer the call? No. Too many people trust Jesus for salvation and His occasional help in emergencies, but little more. Too few of us are willing to sacrifice our selfishness in the pursuit of love. But if we truly desire the depths of marriage unity with Jesus *in actual experience*, we must make a covenant to love Him with all our heart and soul. There is simply no other way; marriage requires covenant.

Scripture speaks plainly about our betrothal to Jesus and our call to become His bride. However, as we will see, many people teach that believers are engaged to Jesus for a future wedding that only takes place in heaven after we die. In other words, we are betrothed in this life, but only married in eternity. But is this actually true?

There are two elements needed for a true marriage: covenant *and* union. We can clearly see the covenant of love within Scripture, but in order to truly know if marriage to Jesus is attainable in this present life, we need to look at what the Scripture says of unity. Does the Bible speak of becoming one with Jesus in this life? Or is unity with Christ something that only takes place at the end of time?

One Flesh

Ephesians 5:25-32

Husbands, love your wives, as Christ loved the church and gave himself up for her, that he might sanctify her, having cleansed her by the washing of water with the word, so that he might present the church to himself in splendour, without spot or wrinkle or any such thing, that she might be holy and without blemish. In the same way husbands should love their wives as their own bodies. He who loves his wife loves himself. For no one ever hated his own flesh, but nourishes and cherishes it, just as Christ does the church, because we are members of his body. "Therefore a man shall leave his father and mother and hold fast to his wife, and the two shall become one flesh." This mystery is profound, and I am saying that it refers to Christ and the church.

1 Corinthians 6:15-17 (NASB)

Do you not know that your bodies are members of Christ? Shall I then take away the members of Christ and make them members of a prostitute? May it never be! Or do you not know that the one who joins himself to a prostitute is one body with her? For He says, "The two shall become one flesh." But the one who joins himself [in intimate union] to the Lord is one spirit with Him.

"The one who joins himself to Jesus is one spirit with Him." In these passages, Paul is writing of our relationship with Jesus in the context of a marriage. Just as a man is joined to his wife and the two become one flesh, so we can become one spirit with Jesus, in our present time.

God intentionally chooses the most sacred and exhilarating act of love as a metaphor for becoming one spirit with Him. Why? Because it conveys a sense of ongoing devotion, surrender, vulnerability, intimacy, affection, joy, unity, knowledge, satisfaction and glory. This is the life that Jesus wants to enjoy with us! And as Paul writes, though this may be a profound mystery, it is an absolute and attainable reality. If we are willing to join ourselves to the Lord, we will become one spirit with Jesus.

True Food

John 6:53-56

So Jesus said to them, "Truly, truly, I say to you, unless you eat the flesh of the Son of Man and drink his blood, you have no life in you. Whoever feeds on my flesh and drinks my blood has eternal life, and I will raise him up on the last day. For my flesh is true food, and my blood is true drink. Whoever feeds on my flesh and drinks my blood abides in me, and I in him."

Here Jesus extends our understanding of unity by calling us to abide in Him by eating His flesh and drinking His blood. Jesus is not speaking in a physical sense here, instead He is using the terms *flesh* and blood as symbols of spiritual realities. When used in a spiritual context, the term *flesh* speaks of our fallen human nature. For example, Scripture calls us to crucify the flesh with its passions and desires.[1] This is not a call to crucify our physical bodies, but to embrace the power of the cross to overcome the selfish nature within us.

But if Scripture uses the word *flesh* spiritually to speak of the sinful nature, what does it mean to eat the flesh of Christ?

2 Peter 1:4

...He has granted to us his precious and very great promises, so that through them you may become partakers of the divine nature, having escaped from the corruption that is in the world because of sinful desire...

Our flesh nature may be corrupted by selfishness, but the nature of Jesus is one of pure, perfect love. To eat Christ's flesh is therefore to take His nature and make it our own.

The nature of a person defines their whole character—who they are, how they think, and what they do. Our unity with Jesus therefore brings us to experience new depths of love, joy, humility, wisdom, and zeal as He shares His character with us. And because our nature shapes our instincts (what we do naturally), the more we share the nature of Christ, the more we start instinctively doing the things which please Him. This is the glorious power of the marriage covenant. It allows the love of God to reclaim the very core of our being and completely transform us from the inside out. In this place of unity, we discover more and more that to live truly is Christ.[2]

Leviticus 17:11

"For the life of the flesh is in the blood, and I have given it for you on the altar to make atonement for your souls, for it is the blood that makes atonement by the life."

In the natural realm, the life of the flesh is in the blood. The same is true spiritually. To drink the spiritual blood of Christ is to let the life and energy of His Spirit infuse our being and bring His nature to life within us.

In Jewish weddings, the bride and groom drink from a single glass of wine, symbolising their unity. In the same way, Jesus invites us to drink the wine of the new covenant—His blood. Every time we commune with Jesus we make a prophetic statement: *"I will be one flesh and blood with Christ. I exchange my selfish nature with His nature of love, and I exchange my sin and brokenness for the life of His Spirit. I eat and drink that we would be even more one together."* Union is the goal of communion.

One in Christ

John 17:20-23

"I do not ask for these only, but also for those who will believe in me through their word, that they may all be one, just as you, Father, are in me, and I in you, that they also may be in us, so that the world may believe that you have sent me. The glory that you have given me I have given to them, that they may be one even as we are one, I in them and you in me, that they may become perfectly one, so that the world may know that you sent me and loved them even as you loved me."

Here again we see Jesus' unrelenting focus on unity. In His final prayer before the cross, Jesus prays that we would all become one with Him. Jesus' focus is not on a unity that is found only in eternity after we die. On the contrary, Jesus prays that the Father would make us one with Christ so that *this present world* may know that the Father sent Jesus and that He loves us like He loves Jesus. Marriage unity with Jesus is both for now and forever.

Love and Unity

Colossians 3:14 (NASB)

Beyond all these things put on love, which is the perfect bond of unity.

Love is the perfect bond of unity. In every sphere of relationship, love compels us towards unity. When a husband and wife love each other, that love compels them towards sexual unity. The love shared between friends cultivates a unity of heart which draws friends to spend time together and invest in each other. The love within a family binds the family together as one. In all our relationships, the measure of love that flows from one to another determines the level of unity.

This principle of love and unity is also true of God. The love shared between the Father and the Son is a love that demands unity. Because God's love is perfect, infinite and absolute, it ensures a perfect, infinite and absolute unity between the Father, Son and Spirit.

This love of God extends to us and compels Jesus to seek unity with us. This is why He comes to us as both a saviour and a bridegroom. He wants to free us from our isolation and selfishness so He can share Himself with us. Our response to Him determines the degree of love and unity we are willing to let Him enjoy. So let us remove the limitations.

The beauty of the first command is that we are not expected to generate any love by ourselves. It is a command that only God can fulfil, so we simply need to ask the Father to love Jesus through us. As we let His love flow through us, it will lead us into a deeper unity with Jesus. As this unity with Jesus grows, our capacity for love will also increase. As the Spirit fills our new capacity, the increased love will then create more unity, which then releases more love. This is the awesome cascade of covenant love. This is our inheritance of life in design. And it all begins with one simple word: *Yes.*

Pray

Father, thank you for creating me to share your love for Jesus and to live in unity with Him. Jesus, please share more of your nature and your Spirit with me. Please show me how to join myself to you in covenant love so we can become more one. I love you.

10 | Preparing for Love

In Biblical times there was often a period of up to a year between a couple's betrothal and their marriage. This gave the couple time to prepare for their new life together. The groom would prepare a home for them to live in and the bride would beautify herself for the wedding.

Over the next few chapters, we will look at other ways we can prepare our hearts for Jesus. We will look at areas such as purity, devotion, humility, and freedom. Before we start, we need to remember that it is the Holy Spirit who prepares us for Jesus. While our learning can be useful, these principles must not distract us from the work of the Holy Spirit. Each day we need to listen for His voice to let Him show us where to focus.

Esther 2:5-13 (NASB)
Now there was at the citadel in Susa a Jew whose name was Mordecai, the son of Jair, the son of Shimei, the son of Kish, a Benjamite, who had been taken into exile from Jerusalem with the captives who had been exiled with Jeconiah king of Judah, whom Nebuchadnezzar the king of Babylon had exiled. He was bringing up Hadassah, that is Esther, his uncle's daughter, for she had no father or mother. Now the young lady was beautiful of form and face, and when her father and her mother died, Mordecai took her as his own daughter. So it came about when the command and decree of the king were heard and many young ladies were gathered to the citadel of Susa into the custody of Hegai, that Esther was taken to the king's palace into the custody of Hegai, who was in charge of the women. Now the young lady pleased him and found favour with him. So he quickly provided her with her cosmetics and food, gave seven choice maids from the king's palace and transferred her and her maids to the best place in the

harem. Esther did not make known her people or her kindred, for Mordecai had instructed her that she should not make them known. Every day Mordecai walked back and forth in front of the court of the harem to learn how Esther was and how she fared. Now when the turn of each young lady came to go in to King Ahasuerus, after the end of her twelve months under the regulations for the women—for the days of their beautification were completed as follows: six months with oil of myrrh and six months with spices and the cosmetics for women— the young lady would go in to the king in this way: anything that she desired was given her to take with her from the harem to the king's palace.

Before Esther became queen, like the other virgins, she had to go through a time of preparation. This preparation consisted of beauty treatments involving oil, spices and cosmetics. At the end of the year, Esther was then ready to appear before the king in all her glory.

The story of Esther is a living picture of our relationship with Jesus. Like Esther, we have been selected to become a bride for our King. And like Esther, we will also go through a time of preparation as we are made ready for covenant love.

Oil of Myrrh

1 Samuel 16:13a
Then Samuel took the horn of oil and anointed him in the midst of his brothers. And the Spirit of the LORD rushed upon David from that day forward.

In Scripture, oil is used as a symbol of the Holy Spirit. Like David, when we are anointed by God, the Holy Spirit comes upon us in power.

In spiritual terms, we start to prepare our hearts for Jesus by immersing ourselves in the oil of the Spirit. As we abide in the Spirit and live in His presence, we are filled with more of the life of Christ. His oil flows into the far reaches of our heart, softening and changing us with His love.

Spices

Spice: *besem*
Spice, balsam, balsam tree, perfume; sweet, sweet smell, sweet fragrance.

Ephesians 5:2
And walk in love, as Christ loved us and gave himself up for us, a fragrant offering and sacrifice to God.

2 Corinthians 3:17-18
Now the Lord is the Spirit, and where the Spirit of the Lord is, there is freedom. And we all, with unveiled face, beholding the glory of the Lord, are being transformed into the same image from one degree of glory to another. For this comes from the Lord who is the Spirit.

The spices were given to Esther to produce a fragrant aroma like perfume. In spiritual terms, the spices represent sacrificial worship and prayer, which rise like a sweet aroma before God.[1]

Worship and prayer can usher us into the presence of God where we can behold the glory of God and be changed into His image. In prayer, we unite our will with the will of God. Through sacrificial worship, we choose costly love and are drawn into intimacy with the Lord. Every moment we spend in prayer and every act of worship adds a fragrance to our lives which increases our spiritual beauty in the eyes of Christ.

Cosmetics

The word *tamruq*, translated as *cosmetics*, means "items for purification," such as cleansing, scrubbing or scouring. [2] Unlike makeup, which is used to hide blemishes and imperfections, it appears that Esther's preparations involved a deep cleansing that removed the top layer of skin and exposed her natural beauty.[3]

Jesus has never been interested in giving us makeup to cover over the imperfections of our heart. He wants to fully cleanse our hearts and wash away all our spots and blemishes in His blood. This process requires genuine vulnerability as we allow God to expose all the things we would rather hide. It is an uncomfortable and humbling process that few people willingly embrace. However, if we let Him expose our sin and bondages, He will set us free and make us truly beautiful.

Purifying the Heart

Some people teach that because Jesus took all our sin at the cross, we are already entirely pure and holy in His sight. They say that we were already forgiven before we were born, and so we must see ourselves as already holy. But are we truly already pure in the sight of God? Or is there a work of purification that needs to take place in our lives?

> 1 John 3:3 (NKJV)
> And everyone who has this hope in Him purifies himself, just as He is pure.

Everyone who hopes in Jesus purifies himself because Jesus is pure. The issue here is not one of forgiveness, but one of purity. In our spiritual infancy, even though we are forgiven, saved and redeemed, we are still inherently selfish.[4] It is one thing to be forgiven of our selfish acts, but another thing entirely to be purified from our selfishness.

Our call is to press on to maturity, not remaining as infants in Christ, but growing in faith and love to become the bride of Christ. This maturing process moves us quickly past receiving the gift of forgiveness and into the purification of our hearts.

> Ephesians 5:25-27 (NASB)
> Husbands, love your wives, as Christ loved the church and gave himself up for her, that he might sanctify her, having cleansed her by the washing of water with the word, so that he might present the church to himself in splendour, without spot or wrinkle or any such thing, that she might be holy and without blemish.

Jesus gave His life so that He might present us to Himself as a glorious bride without spot or blemish. The power of God to purify our hearts is found at the cross. It is the absolute power of His blood to wash away all sin.

> **1 John 1:7, 9**
> If we walk in the Light as He Himself is in the Light, we have fellowship with one another, and the blood of Jesus His Son cleanses us from all sin…If we confess our sins, He is faithful and righteous to forgive us our sins and to cleanse us from all unrighteousness.

In our infancy, we usually focus on dealing with our sin by asking Jesus to forgive us. We deal with sin like a harvest of bad fruit. Season after season we return, asking forgiveness for the same faults. And God always forgives us. In this sense, forgiveness is a gift that is received by faith and requires little transformation on our part. We simply need to believe that Jesus died for us and accept His love and forgiveness.

However, if we are to grow in God, our focus needs to move from forgiveness to transformation. We need to realise that the blood of Jesus is powerful enough to take away both the fruit of sin and all its roots. For the word of God says that Jesus' blood can cleanse us from *all* our sin and from *all* unrighteousness. His blood is enough to bring both forgiveness and purity.[5]

> **James 5:16**
> Therefore, confess your sins to one another, and pray for one another so that you may be healed. The effective prayer of a righteous man can accomplish much.

The blood of Jesus washes away our sin as we bring it into the light. Often it is enough to confess our sin directly to God and trust Him to cut it out of our hearts. However, at times the Holy Spirit may call us to confess our sin to another person in order to heal us. In *First Love,* we learned that sometimes sin can attach to a personal wounding by providing comfort for our pain.

When we confess the sin to another person, the blood of Jesus removes it and the Spirit of God is then free to heal our hearts.

It is important to let the Holy Spirit guide us in this. He will show us when we need to confess our sin to another person and who we can trust to hear our confession. We can think of it like having a splinter in the skin. Often we will be able to remove it ourselves, but at times we may need some help. In these times, we need to reject any shame or embarrassment that would keep us from dealing with the sin. Instead, we need to connect with people who love us and want to help us prepare our hearts for Jesus.

Psalm 90:8
You have set our iniquities before you,
our secret sins in the light of your presence.

It takes real courage and humility to live in the light, but that is the only place where truth is found. It is humbling to confess to other people, and it takes courage to confront the darkness in our own hearts. But God is good and He will share His courage and humility with us if we ask Him.

Sin brings darkness and deception, and so often we can be unaware of the sin we are tolerating in our hearts.[6] We can be blind to our pride. We can think that our anger problem is a form of righteous indignation. We can rationalise our love of ungodly entertainment by calling it the blessing of relaxation. We can believe that our spiritual control is godly leadership. We can honestly think that the pursuit of wealth is a form of wisdom. Every sin can deceive us and leave us blind to the state of our own hearts. Like David, we need to ask God to cleanse us from our hidden faults.[7] As the Holy Spirit exposes our sin, we can then confess it, repent, and experience the power of Jesus' blood to wash that sin *entirely* out of our hearts. And when Jesus washes away our sin, He remembers it no more. Instead, He restores us into true purity and innocence. Through His blood we become like a pure virgin, without spot, wrinkle or blemish; a bride that is ready for her time of love.

Pray

Father, thank you that you have given me your Spirit to prepare my heart for a greater love. I give you permission to go into every part of my heart and soul to cleanse me. I give you permission to expose my hidden sin and bring any agreements with darkness into the light. Let the purifying blood of Jesus flood me and make me a pure bride without spot or blemish.

11 | The Ten Virgins

Through His parables and teachings, Jesus reveals the keys to knowing God in different dimensions of relationship. In the parable of the Sower, Jesus shows us how we need to cultivate an honest and humble heart to know Him as our teacher. In John 10, Jesus shows us how we need to hear His voice to truly know Him as our shepherd. In the parable of the prodigal son, Jesus reveals that to know God as our Father, we need to stop striving to earn His love and just let Him embrace us. In all His teachings on relationship with God, Jesus saves the best wine till last. As His earthly ministry was coming to a close, Jesus gives us keys to knowing Him as our bridegroom and husband.

Matthew 25:1-12
"Then the kingdom of heaven will be like ten virgins who took their lamps and went to meet the bridegroom. Five of them were foolish, and five were wise. For when the foolish took their lamps, they took no oil with them, but the wise took flasks of oil with their lamps. As the bridegroom was delayed, they all became drowsy and slept. But at midnight there was a cry, 'Here is the bridegroom! Come out to meet him.' Then all those virgins rose and trimmed their lamps. And the foolish said to the wise, 'Give us some of your oil, for our lamps are going out.' But the wise answered, saying, 'Since there will not be enough for us and for you, go rather to the dealers and buy for yourselves.' And while they were going to buy, the bridegroom came, and those who were ready went in with him to the marriage feast, and the door was shut. Afterward the other virgins came also, saying, 'Lord, lord, open to us.' But he answered, 'Truly, I say to you, I do not know you.'"

It has been taught that this parable only speaks of Jesus' coming at the end of time.[1] However, if we limit the relevance of this parable to a single, future generation of believers, we completely miss the message that Jesus wants to share with us now.

Jesus started His ministry by calling the people to "repent, for the kingdom of God is at hand."[2] This one statement sets the context for all His parables about the kingdom. The kingdom of heaven is at hand—it is within our reach. The parables that Jesus shares use symbols to give us keys to experiencing different aspects of the kingdom of heaven through our relationship with God. And this parable is no different. The parable of the ten virgins is not teaching us about salvation but about coming to know Jesus as our bridegroom. Within the parable, Jesus gives us keys to preparing our hearts for covenant love with Jesus *in this life*. This makes the parable not only relevant but vitally important for every generation.

The Bridegroom

John 3:25-30 [3]

Therefore there arose a discussion on the part of John's disciples with a Jew about purification. And they came to John and said to him, "Rabbi, He who was with you beyond the Jordan, to whom you have testified, behold, He is baptising and all are coming to Him." John answered and said, "A man can receive nothing unless it has been given him from heaven. You yourselves are my witnesses that I said, 'I am not the Christ,' but, 'I have been sent ahead of Him.' He who has the bride is the bridegroom; but the friend of the bridegroom, who stands and hears him, rejoices greatly because of the bridegroom's voice. So this joy of mine has been made full. He must increase, but I must decrease."

Like every other parable, the parable of the ten virgins uses symbolism. Jesus does not state what these symbols represent, which means we need to search the Scripture to find keys to interpreting the parable.[4] Here we find that Jesus is the bridegroom, coming to take His bride.

The Ten Virgins

2 Corinthians 11:2

For I am jealous for you with a godly jealousy; for I betrothed you to one husband, so that to Christ I might present you as a pure virgin.

Both wise and foolish virgins represent people who have been redeemed by the blood of Jesus. They are all believers who have answered the call to follow Jesus.

Oil of the Spirit

2 Corinthians 1:21-22

And it is God who establishes us with you in Christ, and has anointed us, and who has also put his seal on us and given us his Spirit in our hearts as a guarantee.

Scripture uses oil to represent the Holy Spirit.[5] When God anoints us with His Spirit, His indwelling presence becomes the source of our joy, healing, unity, spiritual prosperity and power—all things represented in Scripture by oil.

The Lamp of the Word

Psalm 119:105

Your word is a lamp to my feet and a light to my path.

The word of God is a lamp and a light. But if the word of God is a lamp, how does it become a light?

In the natural realm, lamps will not give light without oil. Likewise, oil alone cannot give a useful light unless it is used with a lamp. In modern terms, it is like a flashlight and batteries. The batteries need to be used with the flashlight to bring forth light. In the same way, the word of God is lifeless apart from the Holy Spirit. It is the Spirit that breathes life into the word so that together they can bring forth light.

Light

Mark 4:22 (NASB)

"For nothing is hidden, except to be revealed; nor has anything been secret, but that it would come to light."

It was because Jesus came to reveal God to us that Simeon called Him the "Light of Revelation."[6] Light overcomes the darkness and reveals what was previously hidden. In Scripture, light is a symbol of revelation.[7]

Getting Oil

Knowing the symbolism that Jesus uses in the parable of the ten virgins, we need to ask God: How do we apply these keys in our own lives?

John 15:9-10

"Just as the Father has loved Me, I have also loved you; abide in My love. If you keep My commandments, you will abide in My love; just as I have kept My Father's commandments and abide in His love."[8]

Ephesians 5:18 (NASB)

And do not get drunk with wine, for that is dissipation, but be [continually] filled with the Spirit...

Both the wise and foolish virgins had oil, which speaks of every believer having received the Holy Spirit. The difference was that the wise virgins had more oil than the foolish virgins thought they needed.

Our call is to abide in the love of God by keeping His commands and we are commanded to be *continually* filled with the Holy Spirit. A one-time experience of the Spirit does not supply us with enough oil to be wise. Just as Esther received six months of preparation just with oil, so we need to prepare our hearts for Jesus by continually investing in our relationship with the Spirit of God.

Galatians 3:1a, 3

O foolish Galatians! Who has bewitched you?...Are you so foolish?
After starting in the Spirit, are you now finishing in the flesh?

The foolish virgins represent those believers who fail to create a lifestyle of intimacy with the Spirit of God. They may spend time in the word of God, but they fail to spend time abiding in the Spirit and being filled with His love. Instead, they run from place to place, asking others to share their oil. Like the foolish builders, these people hear the voice of God but do not act on what He says. Like the foolish Galatians, they start out in the Spirit but then fall into legalism. They strive to live a righteous life in their own strength, and so trade the grace of God for the dead works of man. This is foolishness in its extreme. Who would ever trade diamonds for dust? Though we may think we are zealous for God, the truth is that when we live in legalism, we forfeit the priceless and become the greatest of fools. And as foolish virgins, if we do not become wise, we will soon suffer one of the greatest losses imaginable.

Thankfully, there is still time. To be like the wise virgins we need to put the first command into first place and develop true intimacy with the Holy Spirit. He will teach us how to come into the presence of God and be filled with His oil. As we invest time in worship, waiting, and prayer, the Holy Spirit will unite our heart with His. He will give us the grace and energy to obey His voice. When we then act with Him, we become truly wise.

Our wisdom can continue to grow as we learn to take the awareness of God's presence into our everyday lives. Throughout the day we can talk, interact, wait, work, love and laugh with the Spirit of Jesus. Or we can just simply be together, communing with each other. Training ourselves to become aware of His presence in our day can take some time to learn. But we are not called to do it on our own. God is full of grace, and He will help us to keep turning our attention to Him. We simply need to start where we are and let Him lead us to live more in His presence.[9]

Priming the Lamp

Joshua 1:8

"This Book of the Law shall not depart from your mouth, but you shall meditate on it day and night, so that you may be careful to do according to all that is written in it. For then you will make your way prosperous, and then you will have good success."

Jeremiah 15:16a

Your words were found, and I ate them, and your words became to me a joy and the delight of my heart, for I am called by your name, O LORD, God of hosts.

Every believer has been given the word of God as a lamp to light their way. As we prepare our heart for Jesus, we need to let the word of Christ dwell in us richly. We need to love the truth, delight in it, meditate and dwell on it, speak it out, and let it saturate our lives. The more we dwell in the word, the more our mind is renewed and our heart is prepared for Jesus.[10]

Receiving Revelation

In *First Love,* we learned that revelation is not about learning something new, but about the truth becoming real for us. When we bring the lamp of God's word together with the oil of His Spirit, we receive the light of revelation.[11] The Spirit of Jesus turns the written word into His living word and makes it active and real for us. He causes it to spark our faith, to ignite our imagination, and to burn within our soul. Through the Spirit, God's word becomes our revelation and our reality.

Waiting

Isaiah 64:4 (BSB)

From ancient times no one has heard, no ear has perceived, no eye has seen any God but You, who acts on behalf of those who wait for Him.

1 Corinthians 2:9 (BSB)

Rather, as it is written: "No eye has seen, no ear has heard, no heart has imagined, what God has prepared for those who love Him."

God has prepared an awesome inheritance for those who wait on Him. The wise virgins had to patiently and expectantly wait on God. Without knowing it, through their waiting, the wise virgins released God to act and bring them into their inheritance of love.

In Scripture, there are many Hebrew and Greek words that are translated as *wait*, and they are almost all positive. When we study these words, we learn that waiting on God is a powerful expression of surrender and humility; one that forces us to stop trusting in our own works and to put our trust entirely in God. Waiting on God entwines us with His Spirit and makes us one with Him. In waiting, we express our faith, hope, and hunger for God as we shut out the distractions of the world. Just as a pregnant mother waits for the time of birth, we wait on Jesus knowing that He will keep His promise and our time of love will come. If we prepare and wait, we will be married to Him.

The foolish virgins assumed that their call to covenant required little of them. They were wrong. Imagine how they felt when they realised the price of their foolishness. The message of this parable is clear. The marriage relationship is too important to miss, so we all must put aside our foolish ways and become wise. We need to immerse ourselves in the Spirit of God and abide in His word. Then we wait. When our hearts are prepared, Jesus will come and keep His promise. So be wise and get ready! Your bridegroom is coming!

Pray

Father, thank you for calling me to become wise. Please help me to bring the lamp and the oil together and to live in the light of your revelation. Help me to be filled with your Spirit and to abide in Your presence throughout the day.

12 | Love and Humility

The bride is consumed with one thought: *How can I love Him more?*

God did not create us to generate our own love for Jesus but to share His love. So if we want to love Jesus more, we need to look at enlarging the capacity of our hearts. To do this we start by looking up.

> **Psalm 113:5-6**
> Who is like the LORD our God,
>   the One enthroned on high?
> He humbles Himself to behold
>   the heavens and the earth.

The universe is made up of countless stars and planets within countless galaxies. As humans, our minds are so limited that we cannot even begin to comprehend the billions of stars in our own galaxy, let alone imagine the incredible scale of the entire universe.

Some of the greatest minds in humanity have spent vast amounts of time gazing into the depths of the night sky. As humans, we exalt ourselves to study the stars. Yet in this passage, Scripture says that God humbles Himself to look at the universe He created. Why? Because God is eternal and the universe is temporal. God is infinite and the universe is finite.[1] God is our spiritual creator and the universe is His material creation. Everything in our universe exists so far below God's eternal glory that He has to humble Himself just to look at His creation.

The humility of God is one of the great mysteries of faith. Having a proud god as our creator would make more sense. We would expect a proud god to create a universe to display His infinite glory. We would expect this god to demand that his creation perform their best to earn his approval. A proud god would enforce legalism in its strictest form. And as his creation, we would have to do our best to obey or suffer the consequences. But our God is not like that at all.

> **Matthew 11:28-29** (NASB)
> "Come to Me, all who are weary and heavy-laden, and I will give you rest. Take My yoke upon you and learn from Me, for I am gentle and humble in heart, and you will find rest for your souls. For My yoke is easy and My burden is light."

> **Philippians 2:5-11**
> Have this mind among yourselves, which is yours in Christ Jesus, who, though he was in the form of God, did not count equality with God a thing to be grasped, but emptied himself, by taking the form of a servant, being born in the likeness of men. And being found in human form, he humbled himself by becoming obedient to the point of death, even death on a cross. Therefore God has highly exalted him and bestowed on him the name that is above every name, so that at the name of Jesus every knee should bow, in heaven and on earth and under the earth, and every tongue confess that Jesus Christ is Lord, to the glory of God the Father.

The awesome humility of God can be seen in Christ. Jesus, the King of Glory, is completely humble and gentle. Though Jesus was (and is) by nature God, everlasting in infinite glory, He willingly emptied Himself of His deity and humbled Himself to take on human form. Breaking all our expectations of a proud creator, Jesus humbled Himself to come and live among us, to heal us and to teach us. He did not demand that we make ourselves worthy of His affections. He did not demand that we love Him first. Instead, He humbled Himself to wash our feet. Jesus humbled Himself to hold back the armies of heaven while he allowed Himself to be arrested, tried, tortured, mocked and humiliated. He then humbled Himself beyond all comprehension to hang naked upon a cross, dying in agony as a sacrifice for our sin.

Scripture speaks of the cross as being the ultimate expression of love. And it was only possible through the absolute humility of Christ. Even though the fundamental nature of God is one of everlasting love, God has to humble Himself in order to share that love with us. As incredible as it may seem, love only flows through humility.

Pride and Legalism

Every day, Jesus continues to delight in humbling Himself. Why? Because His humility opens the floodgates of heaven. It allows Him to pour His love into humanity and to receive the Father's love through us. But this can only happen with our participation. Now that Jesus has opened the gates of heaven, we must open the gates of our heart, and that requires humility.

Because love and humility are such essential aspects of God's nature, they should be the defining qualities of all believers. And yet this is not often the case. As the Body of Christ, our focus has been so intently set on doctrines, interpretations, services, and styles that we have lost sight of the simplicity of humility and love. We have focused on the furnishings without thinking of the foundations.

In terms of doctrine and interpretations, Jesus has made it clear that we cannot possibly understand the Scriptures apart from the love of God, and His love only flows through humility.[2] So if we want to know the truth, the answer is not more Bible studies. Knowledge of the truth starts when we humble ourselves and begin to read the Scriptures through the lens of love. When love and humility are combined with the word of God, they are unspeakably powerful. They are not just qualities of Christ's nature that we enjoy in union with Him—they are our key to unlocking the truth and our defence against deception. When we let go of the protective power of love and humility, we open our hearts to one of the most devastating of all deceptions: pride.

Proud Opposition

James 4:6

But he gives more grace. Therefore it says, "God opposes the proud but gives grace to the humble."

Part of the deception of pride is that we can be well intentioned and yet still live in pride. When we accept any level of pride in our lives, we set ourselves in opposition to God. In our pride, we can believe that we are working for God when we are really working against Him. This became clear to me one day at University when I was working on a computer network with a close agnostic friend. We suffered a major server failure only to find that the previous technician had mistakenly disposed of all the backups. Hundreds of people's work was lost in a moment.

This presented me with an opportunity. If God would resurrect the server, not only would everyone get their data back, but my friend would see God perform a miracle. Then he would have to believe that God exists. He may even get saved.

I decided to pray all night for the miracle. I had never prayed all through the night before and I thought that God would honour my sacrifice and grant the miracle. It was not as difficult as I expected, and dawn soon came, but no miracle. I was disappointed and frustrated. If praying all through the night was not enough to move God, then what could possibly move Him to act? How much more did God require of me?

The next night, I waited on God, hoping that He would give me an explanation. I simply could not understand why He did not answer my prayer. My intentions and actions seemed good; I only wanted to see God glorified and my friend saved. As I waited, the Holy Spirit spoke so clearly it was almost audible.

"Just remember who you are. You're just a boy with a couple of fish and a few loaves of bread." The correction was firm but incredibly kind, and it flooded me with a sense of relief and joy. In those simple words, God exposed my pride and legalism. He showed me that I had been striving in my own strength to manipulate Him into doing my will. My night-long prayer was not led by the Spirit, which meant that it was void of faith and could never be pleasing to God.[3] If God had answered my prayer He would have denied the nature of His grace by turning His blessing into a payment for my self-inspired work of prayer. By praying in this way, I was expecting God to bow to my will and make Himself subject to me. In retrospect, despite my good intentions, it is unthinkable that God would ever answer such a prayer.

When we live in grace, prayer is our constant communication with God. The Greek word for *prayer* is the word *proseúxomai*, which means to "exchange desires."[4] Through prayer, we express our desires to God and surrender them to Him. We then ask God to reveal His will and give us His desires in exchange for ours. When the Spirit of God speaks to us, He gives us the faith and energy to act on His desires.

This took me some time to realise. When I was young, I learned to pray by listening to those around me. I grew up thinking that prayer was a way of getting God to do what we thought was best. It never occurred to me that a central aspect of prayer was about yielding to God and letting Him move me to do His will. Only as God spoke to me did I see the vanity of trying to manipulate God through prayer. God lifted the veil of legalism and let me see the pride that it was protecting in my life. And it was hideous.

By undermining faith and humility, pride was keeping me in a place of spiritual infancy. I was still just a boy. Yet God was patient with me, as He is with all people bound in legalism. Within the correction He gave me a seed of humility and a precious promise: Like the boy with the loaves and fish, if I gave Jesus what I had, He would bless it and multiply it. I almost cried with joy. God is so good. We deserve to be punished and instead He gives us a blessing.[5]

The Journey of Humility

The journey out of selfishness and into love is a journey from pride to humility. For me, I felt like God was orchestrating this journey right from my youth. As a teenager, I remember being asked by a leader to prepare a

Bible study for a small group I attended.[6] I sought God about what to study and felt to focus on humility. This came as no surprise, as I had struggled for a long time with arrogance and insecurity. I wrote out every Scripture I could find on humility. As I looked over the pages, I could sense there was something powerful about humility. It seemed like humility was more than a quality that we find in older and wiser people. Then it dawned on me: God is humble, and it is an honour to be like God, therefore we should prize humility. The call to be humble is not intended to be a burden but rather a profound privilege.

At that time, I did not understand anything about unity with Jesus or our call to share the Father's love for Jesus, nor did I know much of the humility of God. But the sacred honour of humility was impressed on me. I am not sure if it was useful to other people, but God used the study to speak directly to my heart. From that time on, I started to value humility and began to ask God to humble me. As painful as it was, I started to take opportunities to humble myself. These opportunities usually came through difficult relationships or times of conflict. Oftentimes I would be tempted to justify myself or prove I was right, but it was usually all just an attempt to save face. I was scared of appearing foolish because deep down, I really cared what people thought of me. In fact, my identity and self-worth were based almost entirely on what people thought of me. Because my pride ran so deep, there were many times when my pride reared up and added fuel to the fire of conflict with people. However, when I allowed the humility of Christ to come in, I found that the flames of conflict were quickly extinguished. Humility falls on conflict like water on fire and despite what the world may say, the best way to fight fire is with water. I found that humility not only resolved conflicts, but it often left me with stronger relationships than before.

Humility creates space for love in a relationship, but it comes at the cost of our pride. And that can be painful. When I was being humbled, the pain of my wounded pride often prevented me from seeing how God was using those times to change my heart. Yet looking back I know that every time I humbled myself, God increased my capacity for love in some way and fortified my heart against pride and deception. Given the devastating effect of pride on the heart, I believe that those years spent seeking humility created the platform in my life for the love of God to take over. So I would sincerely like to encourage you: *Make this a priority in your life.* Humble yourself and seek humility. You can be sure that love will follow.

Pray

Jesus, it is so amazing to serve a God who is humble. You exist beyond all time and creation; you are exalted to the highest place in all eternity and yet you humble yourself to hear my prayer. Please inspire me to pursue humility. Help me to share more of your humility so that I might share more of your love.

13 | Undistracted Devotion

Psalm 45:10-11 (NKJV)
Listen, O daughter,
Consider and incline your ear;
Forget your own people also, and your father's house;
So the King will greatly desire your beauty;
Because He is your Lord, worship Him.

In Scripture, the Hebrew and Greek words translated as *worship* speak of bowing down; paying homage; expressing reverence; and yielding to the will of the one being worshipped.[1] Worship is interwoven with humility and so as we grow in worship, we grow in humility.

It is important to understand that God does not need our worship. He is already infinite in glory and entirely self-sufficient. Rather, God invites us to worship for our benefit. When we truly worship God, our hearts become one with Christ in His humility. This increases our capacity for love and makes us stunningly beautiful in the spirit. Because of this, worship in its purest sense is a deeply profound privilege. When we worship out of a sense of duty, routine or tradition, we forfeit the power of humility to unite our hearts with God. Our worship must always be a humble, freewill offering of love.

In our modern church culture, we have largely focused on worship through song. We subconsciously think of praise as fast songs and worship as slow songs. Yet in Scripture, while praise is expressed through song, worship is expressed almost entirely through sacrifice.[2] Abraham offered up Isaac to God in worship. The priests of the temple sacrificed animals before God in worship. When David went to make an offering to God, he said "I will not offer to God that which costs me nothing."[3] Worship is always costly on some level. Why? Because it is the cost that creates humility, and it is humility that defines our worship.

It is so easy to believe that we love God because we sing the words of extravagant love songs. We honour Him with our lips and feel emotionally connected to God in our singing, but so often our lives do not reflect the devotion that our songs profess. The truth is that the quality of our worship is not measured by our level of emotion or the sincerity of our singing. After all, what cost is there in a song? No, our worship is only measured by a life of sacrificial love. If we are willing to humble ourselves before God, He will teach us how to be true worshippers—people whose lives express the love that our lips profess.

Imperfect Inspiration

Like young children, in our spiritual infancy we can be self-absorbed and seek God's help simply to fulfil our own desires. As we mature in Christ, we move from focusing on what we can get from God to what we can give Him. In this section, we will look at an expression of sacrificial worship that will help us to shift our focus. But before we do, we need to look at one of the language features of the Greek Scriptures.

Language is the key to all communication. It allows us to communicate with each other, and to illustrate our message. We can use words to paint different kinds of pictures on the imagination of the reader or listener. Well-chosen words can add a sense of life and colour to what we say; other words can make our message feel dry and uninspired. The same is true of tenses in language. The choice of tense can change the feel of the story and engage the reader in different ways. For example, because the past tense creates a sense of distance for the listeners, when comedians tell a story, they will often tell it in the present tense. Instead of saying, "Two men walked into a bar, and one turned to the other and said…," a comedian will often say, "Two men walk into a bar and one turns to the other and says… 'I didn't see it either.'" By telling a story using the present tense, the comedian gets the listeners to imagine the story as if it was happening right now. This increases the sense of drama and draws the listener into the action.

One of the ways that Scripture uses this kind of technique is by using a language device called the Greek imperfect aspect.[4] The imperfect aspect describes a past action in its ongoing sense. Instead of "she wrote a letter," the imperfect reads, "she was writing a letter." In Greek, this tense is used to create a tangible sense of drama. It inspires the imagination and invites the listener into the story. Most non-literal English translations render the Greek imperfect in the past tense and so the sense of drama is often lost. As an alternative to using an interlinear Bible, an easy way to see where the imperfect is used in Scripture is to use the Discovery Bible, which marks the different Greek and Hebrew language features with symbols. These symbols connect to a legend which explains the meaning of each symbol. In the Discovery Bible, the Greek imperfect is marked by the symbol: ⌒

We find this symbol multiple times in the following passage.

Devotion

Luke 7:36-39 (TDB)

Then one of the Pharisees asked Him⌒ to eat with him. And He went to the Pharisee's house, and sat down to eat. And behold, a woman in the city who was a sinner, when she knew that Jesus sat at the table in the Pharisee's house, brought an alabaster flask of fragrant oil, and stood at His feet behind Him weeping; and she began to wash⌒ His feet with her tears, and wiped them⌒ with the hair of her head; and she kissed⌒ His feet and anointed⌒ them with the fragrant oil. Now when the Pharisee who had invited Him saw this, he spoke to himself, saying, "This Man, if He were a prophet, would know who and what manner of woman this is who is touching Him, for she is a sinner."

Here we see one of the most potent pictures of undistracted devotion to Christ in the Scriptures. If we were to honour the sense of the Greek imperfect, we would read:

She started wetting his feet with her tears and she was wiping them with the hair of her head; and she was kissing his feet and anointing them with the perfume...

Here Luke deliberately uses the imperfect tense. Why? Luke does not want to simply inform us about this act of devotion. He wants to engage us emotionally in the story. He uses the imperfect tense to prompt us to imagine the scene and watch it unfold like a movie in our mind. This will give us far more reward than learning about the facts of the story. It will touch our heart. This may be difficult at first if we are used to reading only for information, but if we want to honour the intent of Scripture, we need to learn to engage our imagination. Any time spent will be well worth the reward.

We can begin by asking God to anoint and sanctify our imagination. We can then read the passage over a few times slowly. As we read, we can imagine seeing the woman as she keeps kissing Jesus' feet. We can let the scene touch our emotions as we hear the cries of a broken woman and watch her tears run down her face and onto Jesus' feet. We can imagine smelling the perfume as the fragrance of her offering fills the room. We can listen to the murmurs of the onlookers and sense their discomfort as they watch this extravagant act of worship. We can imagine Jesus looking into the woman's eyes and silently sharing His love with her.

When we meditate on the word of God in complete dependence on Him, the word will do its work in us. God will write His word on our heart and use it to draw us deeper into His love.

Worship, Love and Sacrifice

It was only as I spent time meditating on this passage and putting myself in the place of the woman that I began to understand more of the sacrificial nature of worship. Worship is a costly offering of love that is given to bless Jesus, without expecting anything in return. It is an act of excessive affection that worldly-minded people cannot understand. Why give so much to Jesus?

> Here I am, jar in hand,
> Tears in my eyes.
> I love you so I bow down low,
> And break my heart.

I come to kiss your feet and bless,
 You with my brokenness.
And so I bring this offering,
 It's all I have.

Let my tears wash your feet,
 As I fall down on my knees.
Let my love anoint your head,
 As I worship You,
My God, my love, Jesus.

Let my perfume fill the room,
 Let the voices fade away
'Till all I see are your eyes my king,
 Please hold me in your gaze.

Let my tears wash your feet,
 As I fall down on my knees.
Let my love anoint your head,
 As I worship You,
My God, my love, Jesus.

I sang this prayer many times to God, using the Scripture to inspire me to minister to Him. At the end of one particularly long day, I came before Jesus, longing to find myself again in worship.

"Jesus, I just want to be like Mary and spend some time washing your feet." I did not expect the Lord to reply but His voice came clearly.

"If you want to wash my feet, then for you, the people of Pakistan are my feet."

I had been to Pakistan and had seen the hardship that is everyday life there. Christians deal with persecution, violence and poverty on a daily basis. Many become trapped in slavery because they have no option but to take loans from kiln owners to pay for the medical care of a loved one. The first money we sent to Pakistan was given to a man whose wife had recently given birth, but she could not breastfeed, and they had no money to buy milk powder. Through God's love, we saved a life that day. More recently, I met a Pakistani believer who had been shot twice and lived, and another young man whose father was killed before his eyes by a gunman who opened fire as they were leaving a prayer meeting. If suffering is connected to glory, then the believers of Pakistan must be destined for some of the greatest glory of all those in the kingdom of God. For me, they are Jesus' feet: His bloodied, bruised and broken feet.

The suffering of believers in Pakistan made me think about how we are connected as the body of Christ. No bride would concern herself with makeup and diamond earrings when her feet are in such a state. It makes more sense to heal what is hurting before adorning that which is well. In the same way, it makes sense for the body of Christ to work together to bring healing and wholeness to the entire body, with the highest priority given to those in the greatest need.

That night, Jesus made it clear that if I wanted to worship Him in truth then I would need to offer Him more than just a song. Like David, I could no longer offer to God that which cost me nothing. My worship would be evidenced in sacrificial love.

Without a second thought, my wife Melanie and I began to send more money to Pakistan. We sought to worship on a physical and spiritual level. People are washed by the water of the word, so we made it a priority to translate Bible materials into Urdu. But people are also washed and kept alive by natural water, so we began to fund the installation of wells in villages. Jesus came to set the captives free, so we started the freeslaves.org project with a close Pakistani friend as a way of redeeming families trapped in slavery. Jesus promised to give provision to His children, so we now help families to start businesses that can generate ongoing income. Jesus came to preach the gospel, so we support people as they travel to share the gospel of the kingdom in Pakistan. He calls us to make disciples and so we promote small group discipleship in Pakistan. Jesus came to heal the broken, so our whole team prays for healing, and we also help with medical costs. Everything we do for the believers of Pakistan, we do in worship to Jesus. We recognise that He is present in "the least of these." He is in the helpless widow, the exploited slave, the single mother, the beaten boy, the abused daughter, and the broken father. When we minister to those in need at our own cost, we worship Jesus Christ Himself.

All this started with a short time of undistracted devotion; space in the day given simply to worshipping God and meditating on His word. If we would only let the Holy Spirit ignite our imagination, our heart would grow so much more beautiful and we would find our lives changed in incredible ways. But are we hungry enough to give Him the time? Are we willing to embrace a life of humility and sacrificial worship?

Pray

Father, please help me to read your Scriptures with both my mind and my imagination. Please inspire my imagination so that I can explore some of the depths of your truth. Please help me not to get carried away into fantasy, but rather take me into truth and reality. I want to worship in spirit and truth, so please teach me what it means for me to wash the feet of Christ. May I be a living blessing of extravagant love for Jesus.

Please consider turning to the Study Guide on page 217 and doing the devotional study for this chapter.

Study Guide: page 217

14 | Dying to the Law

Romans 7:1-4 (NKJV)

Or do you not know, brethren (for I speak to those who know the law), that the law has dominion over a man as long as he lives? For the woman who has a husband is bound by the law to her husband as long as he lives. But if the husband dies, she is released from the law of her husband. So then if, while her husband lives, she marries another man, she will be called an adulteress; but if her husband dies, she is free from that law, so that she is no adulteress, though she has married another man.

Therefore, my brethren, you also have become dead to the law through the body of Christ, that you may be married to another—to Him who was raised from the dead, that we should bear fruit to God.

No one can be married to Jesus without first dying to the law. But what is the law? What does it mean to die to the law?

Luke 11:46 (NLT)

"Yes," said Jesus, "what sorrow also awaits you experts in religious law! For you crush people with unbearable religious demands, and you never lift a finger to ease the burden."

At the time of Jesus, the dominant culture of religion was one of hard work. In their zeal for God, the religious leaders taught that the only way to be righteous before God was to obey the law in every detail of life. Over the course of generations, these leaders published exhaustive writings that explored all the different ways that people could break the laws of God.

Instead of empowering people to hear the voice of God and come into intimacy with Him, they filled people's lives with rules, commands, and endless duties. Yet their teachings did nothing to lead people to live a life of love.

As we learned earlier, we can only access grace through faith. By focusing on works instead of faith, these teachers prevented people from receiving the grace they needed for true obedience. Without grace, the people were trapped in a cycle of spiritually crushing defeat. They were bound in a religious system that compelled them to strive for righteousness, while preventing them from ever attaining it. In modern terms, we call this system *legalism*.

Legalism is a religious mindset that shapes the way we relate to God and one another. The main idea behind legalism is that God's love is conditional; He blesses and accepts us when we do good works, but if we fail, He punishes or rejects us.

Throughout his letters, Paul uses the term *law* to speak of this principle of legalism. In Romans 7, he describes what life is like when we live in legalism. We know we have to keep all the rules, but the good things we want to do, we cannot do. Instead, we end up doing the sinful things we so desperately want to avoid. This happens because legalism leads us to trust in our own willpower to do what we think is right, instead of listening to the voice of the Holy Spirit and receiving faith from Him. Without faith we are cut off from grace, and without God's grace, we have no power to overcome the selfish desires of the flesh or to truly love. The result is that instead of leading us into the true righteousness found in faith, grace and love, legalism does the exact opposite: it empowers our selfish nature and leads us into unrighteousness.

The Currency of Works

True effort always flows from love, never to it. When we strive in our own strength to please God, our works become like a spiritual currency that we use to pay for God's affection and approval. We think, *"If only I can pray longer, worship more, fast more often, and study the Bible more, then I will experience more of God's love in my life."* Although we would not phrase it this way, we want God to reward our works. We want Him to bless us when we do well, and sometimes we even want Him to punish us when we fail.

We can see the devastating nature of legalism when we look at it through the lens of human relationships. In our marriages, it can be tempting to use affection to reward or punish our spouse. *You embarrassed me this morning in front of my friends—don't even think about coming near me tonight!* Or, *I'm so touched that you cooked dinner and cleaned the house. Let's make love.* When we give or withhold love based on how our spouse acts, then our love is no longer an unconditional, free gift.[1] Instead, it is a prize for performance. In effect, we prostitute ourselves by making our spouse's behaviour a currency and then requesting payment for our affection. This kind of manipulation reveals a desperate immaturity in our knowledge of love. True love can never, ever be earned. If it is earnable, it is simply not love.

And God is love. He loves us beyond all imagination, and He longs to pour out His love into our hearts. He longs to make us channels of His love and vessels of His eternal glory. Yet, in order to maintain His perfect nature of love, God cannot allow His affection to be earned. He will never prostitute Himself by giving us His affection in return for our works. He is not like other gods. He will not let us treat Him like a prostitute, no matter how hard we may try.[2] God simply cannot turn His love into something that can be bought.

Therefore as long as we are striving in our own strength to please God, we cannot know Jesus as our Husband. Instead, when we place our trust in our works, we bind ourselves to another husband. As a merciless, hateful, abusive, and yet seductive husband, legalism enslaves us in a false covenant of works and locks us out of the covenant of love. The only way to be set free from the prostituting force of legalism is to die to the law. As people preparing our hearts for unity with Jesus, we need to repent from legalism and ask God to destroy every trace of it within us.

Exposing the Lies

Our death to the law begins when we invite the Holy Spirit to expose the presence of legalism in our lives. As the Spirit searches our heart and mind, He reveals the lies of legalism. Legalism has told us that God is not always good and that His mood depends on our behaviour. It teaches us that we need to constantly strive for God's approval and that anything less than perfect, righteous behaviour is failure. Legalism has made us think that we will always fail God, but it is ultimately ok. One day we will die and then Jesus will take away our sin and failure, and we will live forever in heaven with Him.

When the Holy Spirit reveals a lie, He replaces it with His truth. He teaches us that God is always love and He is always good. He never changes, never gives up, and He never fails. The Spirit reveals the nature of love to us and shows us how insane it is to think that we could earn the most precious element in eternity. He sets us free from our striving and imparts to us the grace to receive. He helps us to hold out our hands and to receive God's love, by smiling and simply saying, *"Thank you, Jesus. Thank you that you love me. I receive your love and I give it back you. I love you."*

Ephesians 5:13-14
But when anything is exposed by the light, it becomes visible, for anything that becomes visible is light. Therefore it says,
"Awake, O sleeper,
and arise from the dead,
and Christ will shine on you."

Every time the Spirit overwrites a lie within our hearts, we die a little more to legalism. With every lie that is removed, we create more space for the love of God to flow through us. This process of death will take as long as it needs, but we need to know that it will come to an end. Death is death, not a constant state of dying. If we let Him, God will bring us to the point of total freedom from legalism, and we will awaken to the glory of His priceless love.

God longs for a pure and humble heart to fill with His love for Jesus. He does not want a bride who strives to be beautiful, but one who is effortlessly radiant. He wants someone who is devoted and surrendered to Jesus, one who says, *"Yes, I am yours. May it be unto me according to Your word."* He desires a bride who is free from every chain of legalism, one who responds to His whispers with genuine affection. He desires you.

Seduction of Legalism

Proverbs 7:6-10, 24-27

For at the window of my house,
> I have looked out through my lattice,
> and I have seen among the simple,
> I have perceived among the youths,
> a young man lacking sense
> passing along the street near her corner,
> taking the road to her house,
> in the twilight, in the evening,
> at the time of night and darkness.
And behold, the woman meets him,
> dressed as a prostitute, wily of heart...
And now, O sons, listen to me,
> and be attentive to the words of my mouth.
Let not your heart turn aside to her ways;
> do not stray into her paths,
> for many a victim has she laid low,
> and all her slain are a mighty throng.
Her house is the way to Sheol,
> going down to the chambers of death.

As part of our preparation for covenant love, we need to look at the attraction of legalism so we can guard our hearts against it. Scripture likens legalism to a seducing and enslaving belief-system. It is seductive because it makes so much sense and feels so familiar. The whole world is invested in different forms of legalism. As children, we are raised to expect rewards for good behaviour and punishment for the bad. As adults, we see effort leading to reward in every sphere of life. Our whole justice system is based entirely on legalism. Almost every religion in the world is based on a form of legalism. We even find legalism in many churches. Legalism has made us so judgmental that even when we watch movies or read books, we would rather see the evil characters suffer death or defeat than be redeemed. In our unrenewed thinking, we find the principles of legalism deeply satisfying, even empowering. *Do this and be blessed; do that and be cursed.* Legalism puts the power in our hands. And it feels good.

Babel and Babylon

We can see the attractive but destructive nature of legalism in Scripture. In Genesis 11, the people of the earth gathered together to build a tower that could reach into heaven. They began to make bricks and to build the city of Babel, hoping to make a name for themselves. They were united by legalism; motivated to strive together to reach heaven, while at the same time trying to make a name for themselves.

This city later became Babylon and remained a living symbol of legalism. It was an ever-present threat to Israel, located not far beyond her borders. Scripture says that over time the people of Judah began to lust after Babylon.[3] They coveted the things of Babylon and fell to its seduction. They finally committed adultery with Babylon, prostituting themselves without fee, and the writings of Proverbs were fulfilled on a national scale. The seductive prostitute led the nation of Israel down the way of Sheol into the chambers of death.

It was the repentance of Daniel on behalf of Israel that began their deliverance from Babylon. Babylon fell to the Medes and Persians, and the people of Israel were soon allowed to return home and rebuild. History will repeat. In the end, legalism will be utterly defeated across the globe. The book of Revelation talks about the judgment and fall of "Babylon the Great, the mother of prostitutes." This is not talking simply about a city or country. It is talking about the entire domain of legalism. Legalism is the original source of spiritual prostitution and He is unleashing the forces of heaven against it. And He will prevail.

Until that day comes, each one of us is called to "come out of her" and die to all legalism.[4] This is a work of grace that only the Holy Spirit can do within us. Our part is to repent and surrender and let the Spirit of Jesus set us free. And we can be sure that when the Son sets us free, we will be free indeed. We will be free from all striving, obligation, guilt, control, and condemnation. We will be free to revel in His grace, free to drown in His love, and finally free to be one with our true husband, Jesus Christ.

Pray

Father, I want to be as pure and beautiful as I can possibly be for Jesus. I am so sorry for ever trying to earn your love. I ask you to expose every trace of legalism in my life and completely cleanse me with the blood of Jesus. Please lead me to the cross and help me die to the Law.

15 | Leaving the Vineyard

The Song of Songs is a living picture of marriage to Christ.[1] Solomon is the king of Israel and represents Jesus, who is our King. Likewise, the Shulamite bride is a type of believers who enter into marriage with Christ in this life through faith. They are drawn by God and run with Him. They give their entire being to loving Jesus and so experience the intoxicating love that Jesus and His bride share for each other.

In the journey of love, the Song of Songs starts with the call to die to legalism and pursue intimacy. This call comes to the Shulamite while she is working in the vineyard.

The Vineyard

Isaiah 5:1

"Let me sing for my beloved
my love song concerning His vineyard:
My beloved had a vineyard
on a very fertile hill."

John 15:1a

"I am the true vine, and my Father is the vinedresser."

In Isaiah, Scripture uses the vineyard as a symbol to represent the people of Israel.[2] Jesus builds on this symbolism and places Himself at its centre. He is the Vine—the source of all life and fruitfulness—and anyone who abides in Christ is a part of God's vineyard.

Therefore, on a corporate level, the vineyard represents people who are joined to Jesus. On an individual level, the vineyard is a picture of our personal relationship with God and the fruitfulness that comes from our unity with Him.

Song of Songs 1:5-7

Shulamite

"I am very dark, but lovely,
  O daughters of Jerusalem,
  like the tents of Kedar,
  like the curtains of Solomon.
Do not gaze at me because I am dark,
  because the sun has looked upon me.
My mother's sons were angry with me;
  they made me keeper of the vineyards,
  but my own vineyard I have not kept!
Tell me, you whom my soul loves,
  where you pasture your flock,
  where you make it lie down at noon;
  for why should I be like one who veils herself
  beside the flocks of your companions?"

The Shulamite bride was forced by her brothers to work in the vineyard. She worked through the heat of the day, labouring for her brothers, but failing to look after her own vineyard. Her work left her tired, burned-out, and desperate for love. *Tell me, you whom my soul loves, where you pasture your flock!*

In a spiritual sense, working in the vineyard refers to working among God's people. Like the Shulamite, we can feel pressured by other believers to do "good works" for the body of Christ. Ministering to other believers is normally a good thing to do, but when we work out of a sense of duty or obligation, we come under the yoke of legalism. In this place, it is easy for people's needs to consume our time and cause us to neglect our own relationship with Jesus. Little by little, activity replaces intimacy. We start to feel the distance and so we work harder, hoping that our efforts will bear fruit. Like the Shulamite, in the haze of all our work for God, the vision of loving Jesus with all our heart and soul can quietly fade away.

But Jesus is patient, quietly waiting until we get desperate for love. He waits for us to finally look at our reflection and see how legalism has been disfiguring our spiritual beauty. He waits for us to feel the emptiness and isolation. He waits for us to come to our senses and cry out to Him, *"Tell me, O lover of my soul—where do you pasture your flock? Where are You?!"*

A Different Path

Song of Songs 1:8
"If you do not know,
O most beautiful among women,
follow in the tracks of the flock,
and pasture your young goats
beside the shepherds' tents."

Solomon was a king, but he humbles himself to come to the Shulamite as a shepherd. He sees past her sunburned skin and praises her true beauty. He then calls her to leave the vineyard and to follow a different path.

When we cry out for love, like Solomon, the King of kings comes to us in the simplicity of a shepherd. He hides His awesome glory and humbles Himself to shower us with His affection. Instead of condemning us for our legalism, Jesus simply smiles. He tells us of our beauty. He calls us to leave our life of dead works and to begin our journey to love.

It was no small thing for the Shulamite to leave the vineyard. This was her calling. Her brothers would have continued to pressure her to carry on working as she was supposed to do. She may have been accused of betrayal. She may have had to fight through guilt and grief. But the Shulamite felt the pull of love. She heard the voice of her love calling. *Come away with Me.*

Leaving the vineyard is a picture of dying to the law. It is not a physical disconnection from other believers but a spiritual death to all legalism. It is the end of working for God out of a sense of duty or obligation. It is an end to being motivated by thoughts like *I should, I ought to, or I must.* It is an end to letting the thoughts of legalism guide us instead of the voice of our Shepherd. Leaving the vineyard represents our first steps into a new life. It speaks of being led by the Spirit to become one with the King.

For many people, dying to legalism can feel like entering into a time of spiritual paralysis. We come to the point where we realise there is literally nothing we can do to help ourselves or earn our place in the heart of God. The enemy would tempt us to believe this is a place of helplessness and defeat. But in reality, it is a place of surrender and freedom. Finally, we are set free from the stress of trusting in our own efforts to please God. Finally, we are free to receive His unconditional love unconditionally. When we die to legalism, we come alive to a life of grace and dependence on God.

Every follower of Christ is called to die to legalism. This can take courage. Those close to us may not understand. They may not be ready to die to the law themselves and so they may challenge our choices. But for the sake of Jesus Christ, we must turn our back on all legalism and follow the path that leads to love.

Song of Songs 2:10-14 (NASB)
Shulamite
"My beloved responded and said to me:
'Arise, my darling, my beautiful one,
>   And come along.
>   For behold, the winter is past,
>   The rain is over and gone.
The flowers have already appeared in the land;
>   The time has arrived for pruning the vines,
>   And the voice of the turtledove has been heard in our land.
The fig tree has ripened its figs,
>   And the vines in blossom have given forth their fragrance.
Arise, my darling, my beautiful one,
>   And come along!
O my dove, in the clefts of the rock,
>   In the secret place of the steep pathway,
>   Let me see your form,
>   Let me hear your voice;
>   For your voice is sweet,
>   And your form is lovely.'"

The bridegroom longs to see his beloved and to hear her voice in the cleft of the rock, in the secret place of the steep pathway. The imagery here is one of two lovers meeting in a secret cave, away from the world and its distractions.

Like the Shulamite, we are called to spiritually ascend to the secret place of His presence. This ascent invites us to invest time in prayer, praise, worship, devotion, meditation, confession, fasting, and waiting. At times, it may feel dry and even fruitless as we climb the stairs. Each step can look similar to the last and the enemy can cause us to question our progress. Yet in this passage, Jesus promises that He has a secret place just for us and each step is taking us higher and closer to it. His Spirit is always present, leading us on our journey. He whispers to us, *"Just keep going. The ascent is preparing you. With every step you are becoming more beautiful, more loving, more courageous, more pure, and more devoted. Your Love is waiting for you. You are beautiful and Jesus adores you more than you can possibly imagine. He's waiting for you. You're almost there. I'm with you. Let's keep going."*

When we come into our secret place, we find our Love. His arms are a refuge for us; His wings cover and protect us. In His presence, we have the pleasure of knowing how much Jesus delights to see us and to hear our voice. He rejoices over us with singing and revels in the adoration of His bride.

Marriage Union

Song of Songs 3:6-11 (NKJV)
"Who is this coming out of the wilderness
    Like pillars of smoke,
    Perfumed with myrrh and frankincense,
    With all the merchant's fragrant powders?
Behold, it is Solomon's couch,
    With sixty valiant men around it,
    Of the valiant of Israel.
    They all hold swords,
    Being expert in war.
Every man has his sword on his thigh
    Because of fear in the night.

Of the wood of Lebanon
Solomon the King
Made himself a palanquin:
He made its pillars of silver,
Its support of gold,
Its seat of purple,
Its interior paved with love
By the daughters of Jerusalem.
Go forth, O daughters of Zion,
And see King Solomon with the crown
With which his mother crowned him
On the day of his wedding,
The day of the gladness of his heart."

In this passage, we see the wedding celebrations. The king comes out of the wilderness in awesome splendour to be crowned on the day of his wedding—the day of the gladness of his heart. Jesus will feel the same on our day. When we enter into marriage with Jesus, we will bring new joy and gladness to the heart of God.[3] Our union with God will open new realms of love for us and will empower us to love Jesus like never before.

Works of Love

Song of Songs 7:10-12
"I am my beloved's,
    and his desire is for me.
Come, my beloved,
    let us go out into the fields
    and lodge in the villages;
    let us go out early to the vineyards
    and see whether the vines have budded,
    whether the grape blossoms have opened
    and the pomegranates are in bloom.
There I will give you my love."

In the beginning of the Song of Songs, the Shulamite laboured alone in the vineyard, striving under a yoke of obligation. Having left the vineyard to pursue love, she now returns with her husband. Instead of working *for* Solomon, she now works *with* him. And instead of being exhausted by the labour, she now enjoys his love as she works.

Like the Shulamite we are called to die to the law and pursue the love of our heavenly bridegroom. After we are married to Jesus, we can then return to the vineyard with Him to help others grow in their love for Jesus.

> **Matthew 11:28-29**
> "Come to me, all who labour and are heavy laden, and I will give you rest. Take my yoke upon you, and learn from me, for I am gentle and lowly in heart, and you will find rest for your souls."

> **Philippians 2:13**
> ...it is God who works in you, both to will and to work for his good pleasure.

When we are yoked with Jesus, we become one with Him in His work. And it is easy. The Spirit of Jesus speaks to us and imparts faith to our hearts. Through this faith, we receive the energising power of Christ to do His will and good pleasure. Because we act in union with Him, our work is a work of faith that God will always remember.[3] And because we are no longer working to earn His affection, Jesus is free to shower us with His love as we live and work with Him.

This is the life of abundance that Jesus has prepared for us. But it all begins with a sense of desperation. We need to ask the Holy Spirit to make us so desperate for Jesus' love that we are willing to die to legalism and to take a new path. We can be sure that if we seek our Bridegroom with all our heart, He will be found, and we will be one with Him.

Jesus is waiting. He is calling. Now is the time for love.

Pray

Lord, thank you for calling me into a life of love and unity with Jesus! Please help me to ascend the steep pathway. Please share your grace and energy with me to keep me going. Please help me to get free from the distractions of life and to take the next step higher. Help me to set my heart on seeking my Bridegroom in the secret place.

16 | Sarah Must Die

Genesis 12:1-2

Now the LORD said to Abram, "Go from your country and your kindred and your father's house to the land that I will show you. And I will make of you a great nation, and I will bless you and make your name great, so that you will be a blessing."

In this chapter, we are going to start with some history. Genesis records how God called Abram to leave his home in Ur and move to Canaan—the Promised Land. God promised Abram that He would make him into a great nation through the gift of a child. Abram and his wife Sarai left Ur and settled in Canaan. During that time God again confirmed His promise, saying that the descendants of Abram would outnumber the stars in the sky.

Genesis 16:1-2

Now Sarai, Abram's wife, had borne him no children. She had a female Egyptian servant whose name was Hagar. And Sarai said to Abram, "Behold now, the LORD has prevented me from bearing children. Go in to my servant; it may be that I shall obtain children by her." And Abram listened to the voice of Sarai.

Sarai knew of God's promise of a child, but it seemed like an impossible dream. Sarai was infertile. Because she was unable to conceive, she asked Abram to conceive with her maid Hagar. Abram conceived a son with Hagar and named him Ishmael.

After some time, God came to Abram and revealed that Ishmael was not the promised child. He said that His promise was for both Abram and Sarai. However, not only was Sarai infertile, but she was well past the age of childbearing. Yet this was all a part of God's plan. Isaac was to be born as a miracle child and become a living type of Christ.

Not long later, God called Abram into covenant. Every male within Abram's house was brought into this covenant through circumcision—the cutting away of the foreskin. Because this covenant brought them into a new realm of life, God changed Abram's name to Abraham, and Sarai was renamed Sarah.

Genesis 18:9-12
They said to him, "Where is Sarah your wife?" And he said, "She is in the tent." The LORD said, "I will surely return to you about this time next year, and Sarah your wife shall have a son." And Sarah was listening at the tent door behind him. Now Abraham and Sarah were old, advanced in years. The way of women had ceased to be with Sarah. So Sarah laughed to herself, saying, "After I am worn out, and my lord is old, shall I have pleasure?"

When God promised again that Sarah would bear a son, she laughed at the suggestion. But God was faithful to His word. Even though she was over 90 years old, Sarah miraculously conceived and Isaac was born.

Genesis 22:1-2
After these things God tested Abraham and said to him, "Abraham!" And he said, "Here I am." He said, "Take your son, your only son Isaac, whom you love, and go to the land of Moriah, and offer him there as a burnt offering on one of the mountains of which I shall tell you."

Isaac grew within the family and after some time, God called Abraham to offer Isaac as a sacrifice. Abraham reasoned that God would raise Isaac from the dead rather than break His promise, so he took Isaac to Moriah and prepared to offer him up to God.[1] Just before he was about to kill Isaac, an angel stopped him. Isaac was spared and instead God provided a ram for the sacrifice. Abraham offered the ram and returned with Isaac.

Genesis 23:1-2

Sarah lived 127 years; these were the years of the life of Sarah. And Sarah died at Kiriath-arba (that is, Hebron) in the land of Canaan, and Abraham went in to mourn for Sarah and to weep for her.

Sometime after Abraham offered Isaac, Sarah died. Abraham buried Sarah in Canaan.

Genesis 24:1-4

Now Abraham was old, well advanced in years. And the LORD had blessed Abraham in all things. And Abraham said to his servant, the oldest of his household, who had charge of all that he had, "Put your hand under my thigh, that I may make you swear by the LORD, the God of heaven and God of the earth, that you will not take a wife for my son from the daughters of the Canaanites, among whom I dwell, but will go to my country and to my kindred, and take a wife for my son Isaac."

At this stage, Isaac was in his thirties and unmarried. God had told Abraham that Isaac was not to marry any of the women of Canaan. So Abraham sent out his eldest servant to return to his old homeland and seek out a bride from his people.

The servant, who was most likely Eliezer, took ten camels, riches and gifts, and went to the city of Nahor, a relative of Abraham. Eliezer prayed, and God sent Rebekah—a young woman of incredible kindness, courage, generosity, strength, humility and beauty. Rebekah agreed to become Isaac's bride and Eliezer showered her with gifts. Rebekah left her family and travelled to Canaan. She became Isaac's wife and the mother of Jacob and Esau. Jacob was later renamed Israel and became the father of the nation of Israel.

Many of the events that happened to Abraham, Sarah and Isaac, are types or living parables.[2] Understanding the symbolism of these types gives us insight into our own journey in God.

Offering Isaac

Galatians 3:16

Now the promises were made to Abraham and to his offspring. It does not say, "And to offsprings," referring to many, but referring to one, "And to your offspring," who is Christ.

Isaac was born by the miraculous power of God when Sarah was in her nineties. As Abraham's son, Isaac inherited the promises of Abraham, but these promises were always ultimately for the true descendent of Abraham: Jesus Christ. Isaac was therefore a living picture of Christ, passing down the promise of Abraham to Jesus so that all the nations of the world would be blessed in Jesus Christ.

Hebrews 11:17-19

By faith Abraham, when he was tested, offered up Isaac, and he who had received the promises was in the act of offering up his only son, of whom it was said, "Through Isaac shall your offspring be named." He considered that God was able even to raise him from the dead, from which, figuratively speaking, he did receive him back.

When Abraham offered up Isaac on Mount Moriah, it was a living picture of Jesus at the cross. Jesus was represented both by Isaac and the ram. In Isaac, we see a picture of Christ, humbly submitting Himself to death. In the ram we see the Lamb of God, dying to take away our sin and selfishness.

Two Sons, Two Cities

Revelation 21:9-11

Then came one of the seven angels who had the seven bowls full of the seven last plagues and spoke to me, saying, "Come, I will show you the Bride, the wife of the Lamb." And he carried me away in the Spirit to a great, high mountain, and showed me the holy city Jerusalem coming down out of heaven from God, having the glory of God, its radiance like a most rare jewel, like a jasper, clear as crystal.

Galatians 4:21-31

Tell me, you who desire to be under the law, do you not listen to the law? For it is written that Abraham had two sons, one by a slave woman and one by a free woman. But the son of the slave was born according to the flesh, while the son of the free woman was born through promise. Now this may be interpreted allegorically: these women are two covenants. One is from Mount Sinai, bearing children for slavery; she is Hagar. Now Hagar is Mount Sinai in Arabia; she corresponds to the present Jerusalem, for she is in slavery with her children. But the Jerusalem above is free, and she is our mother. For it is written,

"Rejoice, O barren one who does not bear;
    break forth and cry aloud, you who are not in labour!
For the children of the desolate one will be more
    than those of the one who has a husband."

Now you, brothers, like Isaac, are children of promise. But just as at that time he who was born according to the flesh persecuted him who was born according to the Spirit, so also it is now. But what does the Scripture say? "Cast out the slave woman and her son, for the son of the slave woman shall not inherit with the son of the free woman." So, brothers, we are not children of the slave but of the free woman.

Here Paul likens Ishmael and Isaac to two cities: the earthly Jerusalem and the heavenly Jerusalem. These cities represent two different ways of relating to God. The earthly Jerusalem speaks of legalism—a religious system that enslaves people and separates them from the grace of God. The heavenly Jerusalem is the bride and wife of the Lamb. It is not a religious system but a relationship of love, intimacy, freedom, and unity with God.

Like the early church in Rome or Galatia, so often we try to mix legalism and grace. We seek to know Jesus intimately, while also trying to prostitute Him by earning His love. Paul could see the insanity of it all and made it clear: if we are to live in the freedom of love then we need to cast out the slavery from our hearts. There can be no mixture.

Our Spiritual Journey

Symbol	Stage of our Journey
Abraham offers Isaac on Mount Moriah	We experience redemption as the power of the cross becomes a reality in our lives
Sarah dies	We experience a spiritual death that ends legalism in our lives
Isaac marries Rebekah	We make a marriage covenant with Jesus and come into union with Him

The story of Abraham and Isaac speaks of our spiritual journey from redemption, through death, and into marriage. We begin our journey as we experience the redemptive power of the cross and resurrection, represented by the offering of Isaac on Mount Moriah.

As we walk with Jesus, we then come into a place of death. In many ways, Sarah's life is a symbol of faith and grace, and ultimately that is how she is remembered. However, in the context of Sarah's death, her passing away did not represent the passing of faith or grace, but the death of legalism.

So how could Sarah represent legalism? God had promised a son to Abraham, but Sarah did not believe that she could bear the child. So like Eve, Sarah gave in to the temptation to take the blessing by her own strength. Instead of having faith in God, she trusted in her own works to make the promise a reality and so gave her maid to Abraham. The spirit of legalism always works in this way. It uses unbelief and fear to motivate us to take control. Like Sarah, when we allow legalism in our hearts, we place our trust in our own works and try to prostitute our Bridegroom.

Colossians 2:13-14

And you, who were dead in your trespasses and the uncircumcision of your flesh, God made alive together with him, having forgiven us all our trespasses, by cancelling the record of debt that stood against us with its legal demands. This he set aside, nailing it to the cross.

The cross is not just the end of sin, but the end of all legalism. Through His death, Jesus cancelled the entire record of debt, including all the demands of legalism. To take up our cross with Jesus is therefore not only about dying to sin but about dying to the law. We enter into this death by repenting from our legalism and giving Jesus permission to kill every instinct within us that would seek to earn His love or affection. Through the power of His blood, Jesus then frees us from the influence, slavery and prostitution of legalism.

The name *Eliezer* means "God is my helper." Eliezer represents the Holy Spirit, whom Jesus calls "the Helper." Abraham sends Eliezer to seek out the bride and he finds Rebekah, a type of the bride of Christ. Eliezer adorns Rebekah with a gold ring and with bracelets. He gives her treasures of silver and gold, and beautiful garments. Eliezer wants Rebekah to look utterly stunning when she meets Isaac. The Holy Spirit wants the same for us.

It is the heart of Rebekah that really shines through in Genesis 24. She is extravagant and generous, watering ten camels that had been travelling for almost three weeks. She is strong, selfless, and humble. She is a woman of courage, leaving her household and homeland for a man she knows only by reputation. And she is a woman of surpassing beauty.

This is the bride that God is preparing for His Son. This is you. While you may not know it, the Holy Spirit is your helper, given to help bring out your surpassing beauty. He is making you strong, selfless, humble, generous, and courageous. He is making you radiant beyond words, a bride of extravagant love and perfect beauty because of the splendour which He is bestowing upon you. All you have to do is keep saying *Yes.* Keep yielding to the Holy Spirit, and you will soon be the delight of your Bridegroom. Glory is waiting.

Pray

Father, thank you so much for sending Jesus to the cross! Jesus, thank you for completely overcoming legalism. I want to surrender all my legalism to the cross right now. I repent. I renounce legalism and reject it out of my life. Jesus, let your blood completely wash me and free me from every stronghold of legalism in my heart and mind. Please change the way I think and how I feel so that there is no trace of legalism in my life nor any of its fruits of guilt, shame, condemnation or pride. I say "Yes" to becoming a pure and beautiful bride before you, without spot or blemish. I say "Yes" to a life of wholehearted love. I am your beloved and you are mine.

17 | Let Him

For all the Scriptures are holy, but the Song of Songs is the holy of holies.

– Rabbi Akiva[1]

As we saw earlier, the Song of Songs is a picture of our marriage to Jesus. Just as the whole temple was built around the Holy of Holies, so the whole of Scripture is built around the love that is revealed in the Song of Songs.

In this book, Jesus reveals the deep affection that He has for His bride. It is important to note that in terms of our relationship with Jesus, the Song of Songs is metaphorical and must be applied on a spiritual rather than sensual or sexual level. The physical beauty of the Shulamite speaks of the spiritual beauty of the bride of Christ. The Shulamite's eyes speak of the bride's vision and focus. Her breasts symbolise faith and love.[2] The Shulamite's neck speaks of the bride's will.[3] From a spiritual perspective, Solomon's delight in the outward beauty of the Shulamite is a picture of Jesus' delight in our inner beauty. The Song of Songs is therefore unique in Scripture as an extravagant expression of the emotional heart of Christ. Here Jesus puts His heart on display so that we might see the vulnerable, consuming, intoxicating love that He has for His bride.

Song of Songs 1:1-4
The Song of Songs, which is Solomon's.

Shulamite
"Let him kiss me with the kisses of his mouth!
For your love is better than wine;
    your anointing oils are fragrant;

your name is oil poured out;
    therefore virgins love you.
Draw me after you; let us run.
The king has brought me into his chambers."

The first words of the bride are "Let Him kiss me with the kisses of His mouth!" The kiss speaks of the words and affections that Jesus longs to pour into our lives. The bride wants her love to be free to indulge in intimacy. For this to happen, she must overcome the barriers to intimacy.

Earlier, we saw how the first barrier to intimacy for the Shulamite was legalism. Like people who dig through dry ground in search of water, when we live in legalism, we keep on digging, but we never find the love we are working so hard to find. Only when we give up striving and die to legalism, do we discover that God's love for us is an eternal and unlimited spring; it is a well of living water, under constant pressure to overflow.

But if love is so incredibly good and God's heart is bursting with love for us, then why can it be so difficult for us to receive?

In Canaan, God gave Abraham wells of spring water, but after his death, the Philistines capped the wells. Isaac then had to contend with the Philistines to reopen the wells. It is the same today. Our enemy uses every strategy to cap the flow of God's love into our hearts. He targets us as children for trauma, abuse, neglect or rejection in order to destroy our capacity for love. Yet if we are to become the bride of Christ, we need to let God heal our past and remove every resistance to love. Where Isaac compromised, we need to stand firm and claim our inheritance of love. Every well is ours and they must all be uncapped. We need to be like the Shulamite and call out, *"Let Him kiss me! Let every resistance be removed! Let the wells be uncapped and let the spring become a river! Let my love have His desire!"*

Resistances of the Heart

For so many of us, we have spent our lives building walls to intimacy. We have learned to suppress our emotions and avoid vulnerability. Many of us have had to work for the approval for others, only to fail and judge ourselves as unlovable. Some of us have been hurt by people who should have loved us and as a result, we have connected love with pain. The scars have hardened like walls around our hearts to protect us from being hurt again, but these walls can also keep the love of God out.

For many years I refused to get to know God as my Father, preferring to relate to Him only as my Master. I avoided getting to know God as my Father because, in part, I thought it would require more of me than I could give. I knew that as a child of God, I was supposed to adore my Father, but I did not feel I had it in me. I had grown up so emotionally disconnected from my earthly father that I had learned to run on empty, which left me good at striving but useless at affection. I realised that in order to get to know God as my Father, I needed to be filled with love, but for that to happen I had to let myself believe that God truly loved me as a son. And that was not easy. It was far easier for me to believe that God wanted me to be a good servant and keep striving to please Him. So I closed my heart and embraced the isolation.

Because I had no real knowledge of God as my Father, I could not truly know myself as His son. My perspective of almost every aspect of life was distorted by the absence of this key relationship. The only way forward was for me to begin to grow in my knowledge of God. And that meant I had to lower my defences and let God begin to deal with the resistances of my heart. This is a key to getting to know God as the Father, and it is the same for knowing Jesus as our Bridegroom.

All our resistances to love usually come from some experience of pain. Apart from God, our wounding can create space in our hearts for resistances of bitterness, resentment, unforgiveness, addiction, envy, rejection, and self-pity. Harbouring resentments can be a bittersweet poison. Our selfish nature finds the sense of personal injustice gratifying. The flesh lusts after sympathy and attention, and every injustice gives us another chance to play the victim and receive more pity. When we give in to resentment and use injustice to justify our unforgiveness, we make a treaty with our sinful nature that allows pain to become a part of our identity. The enemy then uses our unforgiveness to block the well of love in our lives. This brings about his ultimate goal of denying Jesus a unique measure of the Father's love. By refusing to forgive others and let God heal us, we put our desire for justice ahead of Jesus' desire for the Father's love. In doing so we cause Him to suffer unimaginable loss.

Any pain from our past does not exempt us from the call to love God with our entire being. God commanded us to love with *all* our heart and He has promised to make it possible. Yet so often the pain of our wounding turns our eyes inward and blinds us to God's vision for love. The enemy then tempts us to believe that we cannot truly follow God until we are healed and so we focus on our pain and search for healing. We think, *"God, when you heal me, then I will follow you and become your bride. But until I am healed, I can do nothing."* When we act like this, we put conditions on our obedience and hold God to ransom. We pretend to be willing, but in reality, our pain is an excuse for not responding to the call of love. Remember the story of Sarah at the beginning of the book. Her life was full of agony and anger, but rather than search for healing, she chose her design of love and God quickly healed her. Like Sarah, if we choose to love God with all our heart, God guarantees to heal us. But we must make the choice first.

The great redemption of the soul is that God can take all the wounds of our enemy and not only heal them but use them to increase our capacity for His love. Our tears can be used to wash the feet of Jesus and bring a blessing to Him. God can forge humility from our brokenness and use it to line our channel of love. Whatever the enemy meant for evil, God can use for good. A painful past therefore presents no obstacle in our call to love, but if we are to use it for our advantage, we must let the Holy Spirit bring His healing. We have a role in our own healing which is to forgive all those who have hurt us. His part is to give us the grace to forgive. As we consciously let go of all the injustice and pain in our lives, the Spirit of Jesus can then repair the damage of the heart and restore our design of love.

Emotional Poverty

In *First Love,* we looked at how we make agreements with demonic spirits that allow them to influence our lives. In the early stages of my walk with God, I allowed my past to limit my capacity for love. But in doing so, I unknowingly entered into an agreement with a spirit of poverty. The main work of this spirit was not so much to bring financial poverty, but to inflict spiritual and emotional poverty. It affected my ability to receive love and to feel joy. Once the Holy Spirit exposed the spirit of poverty, it was easy to break. *In the name of Jesus and through the power of His blood, I break every agreement with poverty. You no longer have any right to steal from me in any way—emotionally, spiritually, relationally or financially. I expel all poverty from my life. I declare that the wells that have been capped will be uncapped and the flow of love restored. I agree with the word of God. Jesus came to bring me abundant life, the fullness of joy, and spiritual prosperity and I receive it all through His amazing grace.*

Resistances of the Mind

In addition to preparing our hearts for our Bridegroom, we need to learn how to lower the defences to love that we have let into our minds. Often we have embraced theologies and mindsets that affirm love in theory but deny the intimate reality. Some of us are taught that we only experience marriage to Jesus after we die, so we reject the call to become the bride now. Some of us are taught that marriage is only for the corporate body of Christ and not for individuals, so we never think to prepare ourselves for our Bridegroom.[4] Many of us have been taught that selfishness can never be overcome and so we make a treaty with our selfish nature and reject the call of wholehearted love. In our legalism, many have believed the lies that tell us we have to somehow change ourselves to be worthy of His love. So we spend all our time and energy on trying to improve our behaviour rather than prepare our hearts.

All the lies we have believed are like a root in our mind that produces its fruit in our thoughts. The root of unbelief produces thoughts that doubt the goodness of God. He may love others fully, but not us, because we are not worth it. The root of legalism produces thoughts that we need to try harder to please God. The root of fear makes us afraid to believe that we can be one with Christ and filled with His love. For what if we believe and God does not keep His word? What if we reach for love and cannot grasp it?

It is time for the axe to strike at the root. It is time for us to invite the Spirit of Truth to overcome our lies, to heal our hearts and to renew our minds. It is time to become the bride.

The voice of legalism would make it our responsibility to remove all our barriers to love. But God is clear: we do not have to take down these walls alone. God has sent His Spirit to prepare us for love so it is His job to do what we cannot. Our part is simply to yield and say *"Yes"* to Jesus. *"Yes, I give in. Heal me. Forgive me. Take down all my walls to love. I no longer resist the call to love. Draw me and I will run after You. Your love is like wine and I am thirsty. Love me."*

Pray

Jesus, you know my life. You know what I have been through. Thank you that you love me anyway. Please help me to take down every stronghold that resists your love. Help me to be vulnerable with you. I give you my past. Please heal my heart and remove every resistance to love. I surrender to you.

18 | With One Look

"I need to love you."

It was more a thought than a prayer, a sense of revelation in seeing the obvious. It came after reading a passage in Matthew.

Matthew 22:35-40

And one of them, a lawyer, asked him a question to test him. "Teacher, which is the great commandment in the Law?" And he said to him, "You shall love the Lord your God with all your heart and with all your soul and with all your mind. This is the great and first commandment. And a second is like it: You shall love your neighbour as yourself. On these two commandments depend all the Law and the Prophets."

The religious lawyers of Jesus' day relished the beauty that is found in the details and complexity of Scripture. Every day they would discuss or debate different aspects of the word of God. However, the details can only ever be properly understood within the true context of Scripture, which is all about God's design of love.

We can think of it like this: Earlier we used the metaphor of a clock to look at the purpose of life. Watches are portable clocks that often have multiple functions, and most are made with a near-perfect blend of hidden complexity and visible simplicity. However, despite the many features and functions, a watch is governed by a single overarching purpose: to tell the time. It is this purpose alone that defines a watch as a watch. If the watch loses its ability to keep time, all its other functions become meaningless.

As it was in Jesus' time, so it is today. There are so many academic discussions that are focused on the complexity of Scripture. Like studying the gears of a watch, we zoom in with our microscopes to study the smallest details of God's word. We study how faith connects with truth and grace; we marvel at how humility works with worship to bring transformation; we wonder at how mercy and justice so perfectly fit together at the cross. Yet rarely do we zoom out to see the big picture—the reason for our amazing design. Instead, the details become distractions, blinding us to the primary purpose for our creation.

In the interaction between Jesus and the lawyer, Jesus helps us to zoom out and see God's overarching purpose for our lives. Like a watch asking its maker, "what's my most important command?" so the lawyer asks Jesus which command is the greatest. And like a watchmaker saying, "Tell the time," Jesus responds not simply with a command, with but a revelation of our design. By saying that the most important command is to love God with our entire being and to love others, Jesus is revealing that God has perfectly designed us for a life of overflowing love.

Everything in the Bible hinges on these commands to love. Love is the context that gives every detail meaning; love is the beginning, middle and end of the word of God. We therefore have nothing to gain from knowing or teaching the Scripture if we are not willing to live a life of wholehearted love.

As I read this passage, I realised that no created thing can ever find true fulfilment outside of its design. And we are made for love. So as a young man I devoted my life to loving God with all my heart and soul, and I trusted Him to make it a reality.

Call to Marriage

When I was 23 years old, I heard a person share about the parable of the wise and foolish virgins, going out to meet the bridegroom. As I listened, I knew that this was my calling. I had devoted my life to love and the marriage relationship with Jesus was the obvious direction for that devotion. So I set my focus on becoming like a wise virgin.

I started to earnestly seek God to lead me into the reality of the marriage relationship. One evening as I waited on God, He took me into a vision. I was standing as a bride in the bridal chamber, waiting for Jesus to come. In my hand I held a flower that I knew was for Jesus. It was white and just a little bigger than a daisy. And it was wilting. As I looked down at the flower, the Father spoke.

"That's your heart. You're not ready."

Through the vision the Father showed me that my heart was far from prepared; I was not anywhere near the beautiful bride that the Father wanted for His Son. Even though Jesus had brought me to the Father and I was fully loved and accepted as a child of God, the Father could not possibly present me as a bride to Jesus in my current state. I had to change.

Getting Ready

Revelation 19:7

Let us rejoice and exult and give him the glory,
for the marriage of the Lamb has come,
and his Bride has made herself ready.

The bride of Christ makes herself ready for marriage. When do we make ourselves ready? *In this life.* The white flower that represented my heart may have been small and weak, but it was pure and real. It could grow. This gave me hope and motivated me to make myself ready for Jesus.

The call to prepare ourselves for marriage does not negate the need for grace. The entire preparation of the bride is the work of the Holy Spirit, but it requires our participation every step of the way. So over the next few months I focused on preparing my heart for love. It was during this time that Jesus gave me the vision written in the prologue. In the vision I saw a young woman who radiated a love and beauty that was breath-taking beyond words. When I looked into her eyes, I could see into her soul, and her whole soul was full of love *for me*. The love that I felt as I looked into her eyes was more intense than I ever imagined love could be. It was a love that surpassed all emotion. I have never before experienced so much in such a short moment of time. In this brief exchange of love, God showed me what love could be like and it changed my life forever.

As a young man, I thought that perhaps my quest for love would be fulfilled both in the natural and in the spirit. Maybe God was showing me my future wife. I asked Him who this woman was and where I could find her but heard nothing. Not wanting to be distracted, I set the vision aside and continued to work with the Spirit on preparing my heart to be married to Jesus.

During this time of preparation, the Holy Spirit taught me to worship and to wait on God. He taught me how to find revelation in the word of God. He also showed me many of the compromises I had made in my life. He revealed my hidden sin and exposed the religious lies that I still believed. I yielded everything back to Him and let His blood wash away my sin, embracing not only His forgiveness but the power of the cross to change my heart.

After some months, I found myself back in a vision of the bridal chamber. This time I was holding a small bouquet of wedding flowers. They stood around 8-10 inches tall. I was encouraged. Progress.

After another couple of months of preparation, I was praying with a friend. As we waited on God together, the Holy Spirit took me back to the bridal chamber. The flowers were now so tall that I could not see over them. I had to look around the side of the flowers to see the door of the chamber.

Jesus arrived. He walked over to me and quietly took out a ring and put it on my finger. I was married. I was my beloved's and He was now mine. Without knowing what I was seeing at that time, my friend spoke a prophetic word confirming the marriage. It was one of the quietest, most sacred moments of my life.

From that time forward, there was a phenomenal shift in my spiritual life. In the natural realm, marriage opens up a whole new life of love and unity. So it was for me in the spirit. After I was married to Jesus, God started to give me wonderful new insights into love.

The Glory of Love

John 17:20-23 (NLT)

"I am praying not only for these disciples but also for all who will ever believe in me through their message. I pray that they will all be one, just as you and I are one—as you are in me, Father, and I am in you. And may they be in us so that the world will believe you sent me.

"I have given them the glory you gave me, so they may be one as we are one. I am in them and you are in me. May they experience such perfect unity that the world will know that you sent me and that you love them as much as you love me."

Jesus started to teach me about how to receive and give love. He made this passage real for me, showing me that the Father loves me just as much as He loves Jesus.[1] The Father sees me as one with His Son, and all His limitless strength is devoted to loving Jesus *in me*. With every revelation came more transformation. Marriage was not an end, but a completely new beginning of life.

John 17:24-26 (NLT)

"Father, I want these whom you have given me to be with me where I am. Then they can see all the glory you gave me because you loved me even before the world began!

"O righteous Father, the world doesn't know you, but I do; and these disciples know you sent me. I have revealed you to them, and I will continue to do so. Then your love for me will be in them, and I will be in them."

The Spirit of Jesus then opened my eyes to this passage. This is Jesus' last prayer for all believers. *May your love for me live in them.* As we learned earlier, in this passage, Jesus is not only expressing the single greatest desire of His heart, He is revealing God's ultimate reason for our creation. The Father created us to be channels of His love for Jesus. This is why the first command is His top priority. The Father wants to pour a flood of His love through us to His Son, Jesus Christ.

This is God's inheritance for every believer. We simply must believe it. The Father's love for Jesus can live in all of us, and especially in you.

This was an awesome promise and God gave me the grace to believe it. I meditated on the truth. *The Father's love for Jesus can live in me. This is why I exist. I am created to share the Father's love for Jesus.* I made this verse my only prayer. *Jesus, please reveal the Father to me so that His love for You can live in Me. Father, please fill me with your love for Jesus. Baptise me in your love. Let every fibre in my being radiate with your love. Make us more one. Let me be a channel of your love.* I wrote songs about it, constantly spoke with friends about it, and continued to seek God to make this a reality for me. Jesus came and died for this. I simply had to know the reality of being filled with the Father's love for Jesus.

On New Year's Eve that year, I was praising God with friends to some music by the Parachute Band. Suddenly Jesus appeared before me in what seemed like an impenetrable light. As He stood before me, the Father poured out His love for Jesus through me. It was like a transfiguration moment; I felt like every part of me turned nuclear, that every atom in me had become a star that was exploding with an inexpressibly intense love for Jesus. I felt alive with love. This was why God created me.

This experience of the Father's love for Jesus was beyond anything I could have ever imagined or could ever describe. It was not sensual in any way—it was purely spiritual. During that time, there were simply no words to think. All I could do was stand before Jesus and let the love of the Father in me radiate to Jesus. It was a life-defining experience of love.

When the intensity of love subsided enough to think again, Jesus spoke.

"I've brought you to the place of being like the woman in the vision, and you weren't even touching me. There are realms of love you cannot dream of."

It all made sense now. The woman I saw in the vision was not my future wife. She is the bride of Christ. She is me. And she is you.

Through the vision, Jesus shared with me what it feels like for Him to receive the Father's love through His bride. The love of the bride fills Him with an indescribable joy and an overwhelming sense of fulfilment. When Jesus looks at His bride, He sees the Father's creation in its full beauty and glory, and it takes His breath away. I realise now how deeply Jesus is emotionally affected by our love. With just one look from the eyes of the bride, the heart of Christ is overwhelmed and completely captivated. Why? Because He sees the love of His Father in our eyes, flowing through the purity of our own unique personalities. And He is utterly undone.

> **Song of Solomon 4:9** (NKJV)
> "You have ravished my heart,
> My sister, my spouse;
> You have ravished my heart
> With one look of your eyes,
> With one link of your necklace."

Though I did not really think about it at the time, the bride I saw through Christ's eyes was only looking at me, staring into my eyes with radiant love. And that alone was enough to completely overwhelm me. Having become the bride of Christ, I experienced a greater love than I ever imagined possible, and yet I was not even scratching the surface of love. I was only looking at Him. How much more intimate is a touch or a kiss? What realms of love can we experience in this life? What realms of love await in the next?

Pray

Yes. Father I say "Yes" to your love, to your design, and to your will. Please fill me with your love for Jesus. Let it flow through every part of my being. Let me be one with Christ in love for your great glory!

Study Guide: page 222

19 | Seeking out the Bride

When the Father poured out His love for Jesus on that New Year's Eve night, I was overwhelmed by the revelation of how much Jesus is affected by the Father's love as it flows through us. For Jesus, receiving the Father's love is an intensely emotional experience. He is wonderfully affected by our love. It is true that when we turn to behold Jesus, His heart is literally ravished just with one look from our eyes.

The experience of that night provided new focus for my life. I realised how much Jesus is being robbed of His bride's love through our selfishness and misguided theology. I realised that the enemy is not just working to keep people from receiving eternal life, but that Satan is battling to keep us from becoming the bride of Christ. If he can shut us out of this relationship then he can rob Jesus of the love that the Father wants to give Him through us. This is his real goal. He hates Jesus and is using every angle possible to stop the flow of love to Jesus. This puts us right in the centre of a personal and vicious warfare against the Son of Love. To keep us from becoming the bride of Christ, Satan focuses on destroying our faith. He lies to the church, telling us that the bride relationship is only for the corporate body of Christ and not for individuals. He lies to us by teaching that we can only be married to Jesus after the resurrection unless we happen to be alive when Jesus comes again. Sometimes he tries to convince us that we became the bride of Christ when we first believed, so we do not need to pursue any greater intimacy with Jesus than we have already. At other times he lies to us by teaching us that Jesus only came to connect us to the Father, so we should focus on the Father and not think about the Son. Satan is using every available strategy to keep us from becoming the bride of Christ because he so vehemently hates Jesus.

We must arise and take up the fight. Jesus must have the love He died for. For this to happen, we need to call forth the bride and let people know about their inheritance in love. As we share the truth of God's design and people take hold of their inheritance of love, we will get to share in the joy of the Bridegroom. And what a joy that is.

Calling the Bride

Through the parable of the talents, God calls us to multiply the gold that we have been given. Our true gold is our love for Jesus. When we become the bride of Christ, the Father entrusts us with an awesome, eternal wealth of love. We can then multiply that wealth by helping others to become the bride of Christ.

The key to multiplication is found in the story of the loaves and fish.[1] A young boy gave Jesus the little that he had: five barley loaves and two fish. Jesus then blessed the food and it became enough to feed thousands. The same principle applies to our ministry and calling. We must start by offering back to Jesus everything He has given us. He then becomes responsible for multiplying it. And He will. He died so that we could all live in love and unity with Him, so we can be sure that He will give us opportunities to call His bride to get ready.

This ministry of preparing the bride for Jesus is one of the highest honours we can receive in this life. Within every person is a channel of love for Jesus that has been blocked up and is waiting to be released. When we call the saints of God to devote their lives to loving Jesus, we become repairers of the breach. Through our ministry, people's hearts are cleared, repaired, and prepared for the Father's love. And when His love begins to flow, it will be absolutely glorious.

We can only lead people as far as we have been ourselves. It is therefore essential that we fully enter into the reality of marriage to Jesus. This will give us a personal testimony that we can encourage others to prepare their hearts for the Bridegroom.

***

It was only a few months after I had come into marriage with Jesus that the Lord spoke and said, "Go to Egypt." He confirmed His word three times. I was 24 years old and had never been out of the country before. God called me to go to Egypt in September of that year for nearly eight weeks.

"I'll need some money," I told God. The Father arranged some work for me to do which gave me enough for the airfare with $500 left over. I caught a flight and arrived in Cairo.

I had been praying a long time for humility and wondered if God had brought me to this country to humble and break me. I was in a foreign country and I did not speak the language. No one knew me here. On arriving I realised that I could afford to stay at the hotel for two months, but only if I did not eat. I expected to be broken.

My only task in Cairo was to deliver a letter written by an Egyptian man back home to his friend who was a pastor in Cairo. The Egyptian mail would often fail to get through, so I agreed to drop it off for him. I visited the pastor and delivered the letter. As it happened, I managed to fix a technical issue they had been having trouble with for a long time. In their gratitude, they gave me permission to use an office at their church and they invited me to attend a student conference on the Mediterranean Coast. Within four days of arriving, I was at a resort, surrounded by people who were hungry to grow in God. I sat quietly and watched the sun set over the Mediterranean Sea. Not broken yet.

One of the people I met there invited me to live with his family. I stayed with him in Faysal, near the pyramids of Giza. Each week, we went to a student meeting at a church in central Cairo. One night I was pulled aside by a man in his mid-thirties called Raouf.

"Will you come and teach the people of Tanta about the Spirit of God?" he asked through a translator. I agreed. Later he told me, "I did not know who you were, except that someone told me your name is Geoff and you are from New Zealand. But God told me that He had sent you here to teach us about the Holy Spirit."

We travelled each week to the city of Tanta, where some university students were meeting to learn about God. The main church in Tanta did not believe in the gifts, power, voice, or presence of the Holy Spirit. Yet for these young men, the Holy Spirit was alive, moving in power and setting their hearts ablaze. He was breathing on His word and bringing them revelation. Each week, people would come with testimonies of how God had spoken to them and shown them that what they were learning was true.

On one night I taught about marriage to Jesus. We then took some time to pray for each other. I prayed for Raouf. In the spirit I saw him dressed in a white wedding dress. It was a surprising vision—a strong Egyptian man with long stubble, dressed in a perfectly white, flowing wedding dress. Jesus spoke from within.

"I'm taking him to be my wife tonight," Jesus said, and I was even more surprised.

"But Lord, it took me months of heart-rending preparation to become your bride. How can Raouf be ready after just hearing one teaching?"

"Trust me," He said. So I shared with Raouf the word that God gave me. His time of love had come. Jesus had taken him under His wing and made the covenant of love with him. Raouf was now the bride and wife of Christ.

Raouf said nothing. After we finished praying, we had some dinner. We finished and Raouf shared his testimony.

"I have never told anyone this, ever. But when I was seven years old, I wanted to be married to Jesus. When I was 16, I bought this gold ring and had a cross engraved on it. I put it on my engagement finger as a sign that I was betrothed to Jesus. Never in my life did anyone share the teaching that we can become the bride of Christ. Except for tonight. Then while we were praying, Jesus told me to put the ring on my wedding finger."

I was stunned. Raouf had spent his whole life preparing as a bride for Jesus. And now, in his mid-thirties, he had come into marriage. I felt like I had been sent as one of the King's messengers into the highways and byways, seeking out the poor in heart who would respond to the call of love. God had sent me halfway around the world just to connect with Raouf, to tell him how much Jesus loved him, and that Jesus had answered his cry to become the bride of Christ.

The time came for me to return home. One of my lasting memories was a note from my translator in Tanta, a young man called Sameh. It read, "Last night Jesus came into my room. He is so beautiful."

Jesus is so, so beautiful. It is one of the most satisfying, profound and joyful privileges in life to watch other people see His beauty, fall in love with Him, and become His bride.

Pray

Oh Jesus, I know how much you long for your bride. I am here, send me. Lead me to your bride and show me how to share this message of love. Help me to call her to the wedding feast. I am willing to go anywhere for the joy of seeing your bride fall in love with you.

20 | Eunuchs for the Kingdom

Matthew 19:12
"For there are eunuchs who have been so from birth, and there are eunuchs who have been made eunuchs by men, and there are eunuchs who have made themselves eunuchs for the sake of the kingdom of heaven. Let the one who is able to receive this receive it."

There are people who have made themselves eunuchs for the sake of the kingdom of heaven. But what is a eunuch? What is the purpose of a eunuch? And what does it mean to be a eunuch for the kingdom?

Eunuch: *eunoúxos*
A bed keeper; the superintendent of the women's apartment or harem; an emasculated man; one naturally incapacitated for marriage or begetting children; one who voluntarily abstains from marriage.[1]

In a broad sense, the term *eunuch* can include someone who is voluntarily celibate. However, in the traditional sense, a eunuch was someone who had been castrated and so no longer had the capacity for sexual desire or reproduction. In ancient times, eunuchs were often chosen as servants in the royal court and were considered loyal, trustworthy and devoted. Like Hegai, who prepared Esther as a bride for King Ahasuerus, eunuchs were often entrusted to manage the royal harem.

In terms of our ministry and calling, we become a eunuch for the kingdom of heaven when we start to invest our time and resources in preparing the bride for Jesus.

Eunuchs were trusted by kings because they had sacrificed their sexual capacity and were not vulnerable to lust. In the same way, we are called to sacrifice our desire for the bride's love. This means that as eunuchs for the kingdom, we do not feed on the affection, praise, or respect of people. Nor do we seek our own ministry or reputation. In this role, we do not let people depend on us, our message, or our ministry. We do not elevate ourselves. Instead, our sole focus is on preparing the bride. We give our best to her so that our King will be blessed. At every point, we direct the bride to Jesus and encourage her to depend entirely on Him. We constantly call her to devote her life to loving Him. We build faith and desire in her. We prepare her with the Spirit and the word. We call her to the cross so that her innocence can be restored through the blood of Jesus. We do everything we can to present her to Jesus as a pure bride, worthy of His love and adoration.

But can we be both the wife of Christ and a eunuch?

Yes. We can all move easily between all the dimensions of relationship that we have come to possess in God. We can relate to God as our Father or as our friend. We can come before Him as the judge or sit at His feet as our teacher. We can rest with Jesus like sheep of His pasture, while also fighting alongside Him as the Lord of Hosts. We can continue to experience every relationship that we have possessed in Christ throughout our entire lives. We can therefore be both a wife to Jesus and a eunuch of the kingdom, moving effortlessly between the roles.

Paul the Eunuch

2 Corinthians 11:2-4

For I feel a divine jealousy for you, since I betrothed you to one husband, to present you as a pure virgin to Christ. But I am afraid that as the serpent deceived Eve by his cunning, your thoughts will be led astray from a sincere and pure devotion to Christ. For if someone comes and proclaims another Jesus than the one we proclaimed, or if you receive a different spirit from the one you received, or if you accept a different gospel from the one you accepted, you put up with it readily enough.

As we learned earlier, Paul had one vision for the believers at Corinth: to present the people as a pure bride for Jesus. He ministered as a eunuch, both by remaining celibate in the natural realm and by preparing the bride in the spiritual. Yet he feared that just as the serpent deceived Eve, so the people were being led astray from the purity and simplicity of devotion to Christ. So how was Eve deceived?

The serpent deceived Eve not only by what he said about the Tree of the Knowledge of Good and Evil, but by what he implied about God. *Eve, there is a blessing in the Tree of the Knowledge of Good and Evil. The fruit will empower you. God is not as good as you think. He is keeping that blessing from you. You'll have to take it for yourself. You won't die. Just reach out and take the blessing Eve.*

Satan deceived Eve with both legalism and license. He first caused Eve to doubt the all-loving nature of God. He then used legalism to convince her that she needed to use her own strength to attain a blessing from God. He used license to suggest that there would be no consequences for her actions, saying, *"You surely will not die!"* The result was that by acting in their own strength, Adam and Eve violated both the will and the grace of God. Even though their motives were for good, Adam and Eve broke their union with God and let Satan sow in them the seed of a new identity. This identity was a new nature of selfishness, sin and independence.

All through the ages the enemy has been using the same deceptions to separate the bride from her Bridegroom. Paul and the other apostles were preaching a gospel of love and grace, labouring to present Jesus with a bride without spot or blemish. However, the enemy was also at work, defiling the bride by preaching a different gospel, a different faith, and a different Jesus.

As it was in the day of the early church, so legalism and license are still being taught today, often by sincere and well-intentioned teachers. Both legalism and license proclaim a different gospel. Legalism states that we need to earn our salvation; license states that God has forgiven all sin forever, so sin is no longer of any consequence. Both focus on heaven as the goal of salvation rather than on preparing the bride for Jesus. Neither is faithful to God's covenant of love.

Legalism and license both twist the true nature of God and so preach a different Jesus. Legalism preaches a Jesus that only loves us when we perform well and is quick to judge and condemn us when we sin. License preaches a Jesus that is so in love with us that He never convicts us of sin or calls us to repent.

If we are to prepare the bride for Jesus then we need to preach the real Jesus, and we can only preach the real Jesus if we know Him. We need to cultivate a relationship of intimacy with Jesus through His Spirit and His word so that we can faithfully share Him with others. The real Jesus is the lamb who died to take away the sin of the world. He is the light of revelation, who came to reveal the Father so that the Father's love could live in us. He is the bridegroom who longs to be one with His bride. He is the judge who purifies the heart of His beloved. He is the king who reigns forever with His bride by His side. He is the consuming fire, who will burn as a fire of love within us for all eternity. He is our Lord. He is the Alpha and Omega, our beginning and end. He died and was raised on the third day and He has become our resurrection and He is our life. He is our salvation, righteousness and wisdom from God. He is the way, the truth and the life. He is our humility. He is our zeal. He is our creator and our perfection. Jesus Christ is the living God and He alone is the lover of our souls.

May we be ever faithful to preach this Jesus to all the nations of the world. May people everywhere hear this message of love and embrace their design and be filled with the Father's love for Jesus!

The Invitation

Luke 14:16-24

But he [Jesus] said to him, "A man once gave a great banquet and invited many. And at the time for the banquet he sent his servant to say to those who had been invited, 'Come, for everything is now ready.' But they all alike began to make excuses. The first said to him, 'I have bought a field, and I must go out and see it. Please have me excused.' And another said, 'I have bought five yoke of oxen, and I go to examine them. Please have me excused.' And another said, 'I have married a wife, and therefore I cannot come.' So the servant came and reported these things to his master. Then the master of the house became angry and said to his servant, 'Go out quickly to the streets and lanes of the city, and bring in the poor and crippled and blind and lame.' And the servant said, 'Sir, what you commanded has been done, and still there is room.' And the master said to the servant, 'Go out to the highways and hedges and compel people to come in, that my house may be filled. For I tell you, none of those men who were invited shall taste my banquet.'"

When Jesus first spoke this parable, He used it to show how the Jewish people were rejecting the call of love and so the non-Jewish nations would be called into love and unity with Christ. Yet the symbolism extends far beyond the realms of Jews and Gentiles. It is a teaching for the entire body of Christ *at this time*. Right now, God is sending out His messengers to call His people into the marriage relationship with His Son. Right now, every believer needs to make a choice whether or not to accept the invitation.

When God sends us out, we need to prepare for a heart-rending reality: many who are called to the wedding will make excuses and break the heart of God. If we are to help people to accept the invitation, we need to see how the pleasures and distractions of this life compete with our call to intimacy. Our wealth demands our attention. Our work demands our time and energy. Our possessions need us to look after them. All the movies, TV shows, social media and internet need our time in order to exist. Our only mission in this life is to love, but we need time in which to love. So when the distractions of the world compete for our time, they also compete for our love. And when they compete for our love, they compete for our very life. If we are to help people answer the call to love, we need to help them value their time and fight the world for it.

Many years ago, a friend described to me his thoughts concerning the things of the world.

"It's like you're on a journey to this amazing place and by the road there's a shiny wrapper. And you stop, and you stoop down, and you stare at it. You know it's rubbish, but you can't help it. It's shiny. So you just stop and stare."

All the excuses that the people made were like this. *I'm sorry, I can't come to the wedding. I have to look at this shiny wrapper.* One day we will see that the shiny wrapper is simply empty rubbish and then it could be too late. If we have not already said *Yes* to the call of love, then we need to act now. We need to put first things first and make the greatest command our greatest priority in life. We then need to put the second command in second place. Having devoted our lives to love, we need to ensure that the everyday affairs of life do not become affairs of the heart. Everything must be kept in a godly balance. We simply cannot afford to be distracted away from our calling to become the bride of Christ. We must accept the invitation and begin the preparation. Love awaits.

Pray

Lord Jesus, I hear your call. I surrender my desires to seek my own ministry or reputation. I do not want fame or success; I only want you. Let us live in an incredible union of love. May it be unthinkable that I would ever distract your bride away from you. Instead, may I inspire her to love you with all her heart. May I compel her to make an exclusive marriage covenant with you. Please make me a eunuch to prepare a bride for your Son.

21 | Bride or Babe?

Before God sends us out to call His bride to the wedding feast, we need to prepare. In our search for the bride, we may find people who are trapped in a theology that denies their call to union with Christ in this life. We need to understand these theologies and know how to answer them.

> **Exodus 4:24-26**
> At a lodging place on the way the LORD met him and sought to put him to death. Then Zipporah took a flint and cut off her son's foreskin and touched Moses' feet with it and said, "Surely you are a bridegroom of blood to me!" So he let him alone. It was then that she said, "A bridegroom of blood," because of the circumcision.

As I was going through the journey of the bride, God gave me a vision of a group of university students meeting fortnightly, starting with worship and then dividing into five small groups for a Bible study. I approached the pastors of the church I was attending and shared the vision. One of the pastors had received the exact same vision from God and so I began the group. Together with four other leaders, we ran a series on preparing the tabernacle of the heart.

At one point, we did a study on the story of Zipporah and Moses. We looked at the connection between the circumcision of the heart and the wholehearted love that the bride has for Jesus. We learned how we can know Jesus as our Bridegroom of Blood. He is the One who shed His blood to circumcise our hearts and bring us into covenant love and unity with Him. During the study, we made time for people to devote their hearts as a bride to Jesus.

This teaching did not please the pastors. I was asked to meet with the pastoral team who had brought in a theologian from the local seminary. We discussed the teaching of the bride on a theological level. As we talked, they voiced one of their key objections.

"The marriage relationship is *not* a relationship for individuals. This is a relationship between Jesus and the corporate Church," one pastor said. The others agreed and I had no answer. I left the meeting a little confused. They were so much more experienced in the faith. Could they possibly be right? Could the marriage relationship be reserved only for the corporate Church?

When I arrived home, I took it all before God in prayer.

"God! What's the story? Is this for individuals?" The Spirit replied with almost audible clarity. Immediately within my heart, I heard the words, "1 Corinthians 6:17." It felt like God was giving His final word on the matter. I opened my Bible, not sure of what I would find.

1 Corinthians 6:17 (NASB)
But the one who joins himself to the Lord is one spirit with Him.

The one who joins himself in intimate union to Jesus is one spirit with Him. *The one.*

In any sphere of life, the corporate experience is simply the sum of our individual experiences. In other words, when we meet together with others, our combined experience as individuals determines the overall corporate experience. So it is with becoming the bride of Christ. It is the call of every believer—the entire body of Christ—to know the love of their Bridegroom. But it will only be as the majority of individuals enter this experience through faith that the corporate Church will come into her identity as the Bride of Christ. This makes it essential that the call to marriage goes out to every believer.

Already the Bride?

"I don't need to hear someone tell me how to become the bride of Christ—I am already married to Him!"

I remember reading a statement like this. It is common in some Christian circles to teach that Jesus is the bridegroom and husband of all believers from the moment we first believe, and that we are all the bride of Christ, regardless of faith or maturity. People who believe in the universal Bride see the idea that we need to prepare our hearts for marriage to Jesus as a denial of grace and the finished work of the cross. *Jesus did all the work and so there is nothing we need to do to know Him as our husband. It is a relationship of grace, and so we cannot earn our place as the bride through our works. Instead, we just need to believe what is already true: you are already the bride because that is how Jesus sees you.*

It is true that we cannot earn grace through our works and nothing we can do can earn our place as the bride of Christ. But our call to prepare our hearts for marriage to Jesus is not a call to earn grace. That has always been impossible. Instead, it is a call to receive God's grace through faith and work with Him as He changes our hearts.[1] This work of preparation is not at all like the striving of legalism. Rather, it is a work of love that flows from grace.[2]

Assumption and Belief

The Universal-Bride teaching puts all its emphasis on believing. It assumes that we can experience the joy of knowing Jesus as our bridegroom simply by believing that we are already His bride. *You are the bride! If you only believed it, it would be real for you. You just need to believe.*

This assumption shifts our focus away from God and quietly places the burden upon us to lead ourselves into reality. There is no sense of journey from revelation to reality or of growing from infancy to maturity. There is no recognition of the need for covenant or to devote our lives to keeping the first command.[3] There is no dependence on the voice of the Holy Spirit as He prepares us for love. There is no call to invest in a living relationship with Jesus. Sermon after sermon, there is only the constant call to believe harder.[4]

Inheritance and Possession

Those who follow this teaching think of our identity as the bride of Christ in the same way as our identity as children of God. When we are born again, we become children of God and we always will be His children. The same logic is applied to the bride—when we are born again, we become the bride of Christ and we will always be His bride. And on the surface, it makes sense.

However, we cannot think of our identity as the bride in this way because by definition, **a bride is someone who is getting ready for marriage.**[5] To say that everyone is the bride from the moment they first believe is to deny the meaning of the word *bride*. We would not say we were teachers if we did not teach. We would not call ourselves prophets if we never prophesied. So how can we call ourselves the bride of Christ if we are not actively preparing to be married to Jesus? How can we call Jesus our husband if we have never made a covenant of love with Him?

The problem at the heart of the Universal-Bride teaching is a failure to understand the difference between our inheritance and our possession. Our inheritance in Christ consists of all the blessings and relationships that God has in store for us, but that we are yet to actually experience. Our possession is everything of our inheritance that we personally experience now. In simple terms, inheritance is the theory and possession is our reality.

At the very beginning of our walk with Jesus, we know Him as our redeemer but little else. As infants in Christ, all the other dimensions of relationship, including marriage, are a part of our inheritance that we need to journey into before they become our reality.

We can see this in a natural example. In ancient times, marriages were often used to unite families and kingdoms. Such marriages were arranged by the parents of the couple, and a child could be destined to marriage even from birth. However, that marriage only became a reality once the child had matured and was ready to get married. So it is with us. As spiritual newborns, our Father sets us apart for a future marriage. He reserves us exclusively for Jesus, who will one day become our heavenly husband.

Therefore, knowing Jesus as our spiritual husband is not something that we experience when we are first born again. The marriage relationship is built upon a covenant of love, in which we devote our lives to loving Jesus with our entire being and living in unity with Him. This level of exclusive devotion to Jesus is not usually found in newborns but rather comes through a process of maturity.

We would not encourage our own children to call themselves a bride when they are only infants because they are not yet at the age of marriage. Yet this is exactly what the Universal-Bride teaching does: it tells all believers that they are already the bride and wife of Christ regardless of their level of maturity and their actual spiritual experience. Telling new believers that they already love Jesus with their entire being and are already mature makes no sense and can only lead to confusion. Scripture says that we should not awaken love before its time, and we should not be telling infants that they are already the bride of Christ.[6] To do so can have devastating results.

Consequences

Revelation 3:14-19

"And to the angel of the church in Laodicea write: 'The words of the Amen, the faithful and true witness, the beginning of God's creation.

"'I know your works: you are neither cold nor hot. Would that you were either cold or hot! So, because you are lukewarm, and neither hot nor cold, I will spit you out of my mouth. For you say, I am rich, I have prospered, and I need nothing, not realising that you are wretched, pitiable, poor, blind, and naked. I counsel you to buy from me gold refined by fire, so that you may be rich, and white garments so that you may clothe yourself and the shame of your nakedness may not be seen, and salve to anoint your eyes, so that you may see. Those whom I love, I reprove and discipline, so be zealous and repent."

People do not pursue that which they believe they already possess. The Laodiceans believed they were rich and prosperous and so they had no reason to seek true wealth from God. For why seek what you already have?

When people are taught that everyone is the bride of Christ from the moment they first believe, their hearts become closed to the message of the bride. They simply see no need to prepare for something they believe they already possess.

The result is that the Universal-Bride doctrine robs people of the faith and desire they need to experience marriage with Jesus. This then prevents Jesus from receiving a unique measure of the Father's love that flows through His bride.[7] For this reason alone, the Universal-Bride doctrine must be exposed, challenged and overcome.

The truth is that it takes a combination of desire, grace, faith, covenant and obedience to possess our inheritance as the bride of Christ. Just as Ruth risked everything to seek out marriage to Boaz, so we need to give our all in pursuing our love. Like Esther, we need to invest time in preparing our hearts for our King. Like the wise virgins, we need to bring the lamp of the word together with the oil of the Spirit, receive the light of revelation and actively wait for Jesus. Like the Shulamite, we need to die to the law and fall in love with our Bridegroom. This is all God's work, but He wants our participation every step of the way. Our part is to work with Him and to delight the Father by saying *Yes* to His Son. His part is to lead us through the process of preparation. And it will not take forever. Very soon, we will come into our time of love. Jesus will be captured by our beauty and He will spread His wing over us. He will make His covenant with us and take us as His own. He will speak to us and confirm that we are married to Him, and no one will ever be able to take us out of His arms.

Pray

Lord Jesus, I pray for your bride. Please set her free from every lie of the enemy. Please raise up an army of love-struck teachers who will go into battle for the bride and teach the truth that sets your people free! May they call people to devote their lives to love and to prepare for their Bridegroom. Let your call of love resound around the world and let your bride arise!

22 | Bride to Be?

Revelation 21:9b
"Come, I will show you the Bride, the wife of the Lamb."

Because the final chapters of Revelation speak of the bride of Christ, many people teach that this relationship can only be experienced after we die or when Jesus comes again. They believe that everyone who follows Jesus will become His bride at the end of time, regardless of faith, maturity or response. Until then, we are all betrothed but not married; devoted but not united.

This teaching goes directly against passages in Hosea, Isaiah, Jeremiah, Ezekiel, Romans, 2 Corinthians, and Ephesians, where God is presented as being a husband to His people.[1] Having once been a husband is God now only a fiancé to His people? Have we less of God's love in the new covenant than in the old? No! Jesus is a husband to those who would be His bride, both in this life and in the life to come.

1 Corinthians 6:17
But he who is joined to the Lord becomes one spirit with him.

We can test this Bride-to-Be teaching against Scripture. Here it fails to align with the Scripture that says Jesus is "one spirit" with us in the same way that a man and woman become intimately one. This is a level of unity that is only truly found in the marriage covenant. If it only happens at the end of time, then why does Scripture speak of being one with Christ now?

John 17:20-23
"I do not ask for these only, but also for those who will believe in me through their word, that they may all be one, just as you, Father, are in me, and I in you, that they also may be in us, so that the world may

believe that you have sent me. The glory that you have given me I have given to them, that they may be one even as we are one, I in them and you in me, that they may become perfectly one, so that the world may know that you sent me and loved them even as you loved me."

As we learned earlier, Jesus prays that we would be one in Him so that *this present world* may know that the Father sent Jesus and that He loves us as much as He loves Jesus.[2] Jesus is not withholding intimate love or unity until after we die. Rather, He is bringing His bride into the glory of covenant love so that this world can see just how much God loves us.

Rethinking Revelation

Revelation 19:7
Let us rejoice and exult
and give him the glory,
for the marriage of the Lamb has come,
and his Bride has made herself ready...

Jesus calls us into covenant love in this life. But does the idea of being married to Jesus in our present time contradict the great marriage supper of the Lamb at the end of all time and history?

No. The wedding feast of the Lamb spoken of in Revelation is a reality and it will be more awesome than we can possibly imagine. But this does not mean that we need to wait until the end of time to know Jesus as our husband. The bride both prepares herself and becomes one with Christ *in this life*. This union is then celebrated for all eternity.

1 Peter 4:17
For it is time for judgment to begin at the household of God; and if it begins with us, what will be the outcome for those who do not obey the gospel of God?

1 Corinthians 11:31-32

But if we judged ourselves truly, we would not be judged. But when we are judged by the Lord, we are disciplined so that we may not be condemned along with the world.

Our call is to honour the word of God and let it shape our beliefs rather than impose our beliefs on the word. People who hold a future-only perspective on marriage to Jesus need to be challenged to find a position that harmonises Revelation with the rest of Scripture and allows for both present and future realities. Most people already do this in many ways. For example, judgment is a clear theme throughout the book of Revelation. Yet other Scriptures talk about judgment as something that we can experience in this life.[3] There is a day of judgment in the eternal realm, which requires no faith to experience, and there is also a judgment in the temporal realm that we can experience through faith.[4] We do not have to wait until we die to be judged by God. It can be both now and later. In fact, the best way to prepare for the future judgment is to earnestly seek God's judgment in our present lives.

It is the same for the wedding feast. There will be a wedding feast for the bride at the end of time, but this does not negate the present experience. Right now, we all have the opportunity of becoming the bride of Christ through faith. This is the best preparation that we could ever do for the future marriage celebration of the Lamb and His bride. Let us make a covenant and become one with Him!

The Need to Prepare

Those who hold the Bride-to-Be position, usually teach that every believer will be the bride in eternity, regardless of how they lived life on this earth. For these teachers, the glory of the bride of Christ is one of the rewards of salvation. But does Scripture actually say this?

Revelation 19:7-9

Let us rejoice and exult
  and give him the glory,

for the marriage of the Lamb has come,
and his Bride has made herself ready;
it was granted her to clothe herself
with fine linen, bright and pure"—
for the fine linen is the righteous deeds of the saints.

And the angel said to me, "Write this: Blessed are those who are invited to the marriage supper of the Lamb." And he said to me, "These are the true words of God."

This passage says that the bride has "made herself ready." If we all ultimately become the bride of Christ, then what need is there for the bride to make herself ready?

The Bible shows that we need to mature out of our infancy and prepare ourselves to become the bride. Marriage is a relationship, not a reward. And just like in the natural realm, there is a process to getting ready for marriage.

If people with a future-oriented perspective on marriage to Jesus accept that we need to prepare as a bride, we can then ask: *How do we prepare as a bride and when does this happen?*

The reality is that we can only prepare as a bride for Jesus in this life. After we die, there is no more faith and it is simply too late. And what does it mean to make ourselves ready? It is simply to prepare our hearts by committing to love Jesus with our entire being, to obey His voice, and to live in union with Him.

Formal Dress Required

The universal, future-oriented perspective on the bride of Christ gives people a false security regarding their place as the bride and undermines the call of selfless love. For if we are all going to experience the depths of covenant love with Jesus later, then why not live for ourselves now? The reality is that we only take into eternity that which we have attained in this life. If we want to pass into eternity in the full glory of the bride, it is essential that we come to know Jesus as our husband in this life.

142

The following parable highlights the need to prepare our hearts for Jesus.

Matthew 22:1-14

And again Jesus spoke to them in parables, saying, "The kingdom of heaven may be compared to a king who gave a wedding feast for his son, and sent his servants to call those who were invited to the wedding feast, but they would not come. Again he sent other servants, saying, 'Tell those who are invited, "See, I have prepared my dinner, my oxen and my fat calves have been slaughtered, and everything is ready. Come to the wedding feast."' But they paid no attention and went off, one to his farm, another to his business, while the rest seized his servants, treated them shamefully, and killed them. The king was angry, and he sent his troops and destroyed those murderers and burned their city. Then he said to his servants, 'The wedding feast is ready, but those invited were not worthy. Go therefore to the main roads and invite to the wedding feast as many as you find.' And those servants went out into the roads and gathered all whom they found, both bad and good. So the wedding hall was filled with guests.

"But when the king came in to look at the guests, he saw there a man who had no wedding garment. And he said to him, 'Friend, how did you get in here without a wedding garment?' And he was speechless. Then the king said to the attendants, 'Bind him hand and foot and cast him into the outer darkness. In that place there will be weeping and gnashing of teeth.' For many are called, but few are chosen."

In this parable, many people attended the wedding but there was a man there who was not dressed in appropriate wedding garments. He was cast out of the wedding celebrations and left alone to weep in the darkness.

Clothing in Scripture speaks of the spiritual state of the heart. For example, sackcloth symbolises a heart that is being humbled or is in mourning.[5] Linen represents a righteous heart.[6] Wool is used to speak of a heart that is striving in works.[7] Each item of the armour of light refers to a different spiritual reality that we can experience in our hearts.[8]

The man who attended the wedding feast without the right clothes is a picture of people who accept the invitation to come to the wedding but fail to prepare their hearts. Like foolish virgins, they do not put the first command in first place in their lives. They cultivate a selfish spirituality, gladly accepting the blessings of God, but then living as containers rather than channels of that blessing. Believing that God's blessings justify their selfish lifestyles, they foolishly bury their gold talent in their own lives. Instead of clothing themselves in glorious love, they dress in the rags of selfishness and yet still presume to attend the great wedding.

One day, they will realise what they have forfeited and what they have caused Jesus to forfeit. On that day they will be overcome with grief. Jesus does not want anyone to experience such pain, so He gives us a clear warning: **Do not take this call casually.** Prepare your heart. Invest time in clothing your heart in the best wedding garments. Clothe yourself in humility. Put on the linen of righteousness. Wrap yourself in zeal. Gird yourself with faith and truth. Above everything else, put on selfless love. Put on love! Do not be like those who are so caught up in the world or trapped in religious beliefs that they reject the call of love. Instead, focus your hearts on your Bridegroom. Make the covenant of first love and then let the Spirit prepare you. Hear and obey His voice, abide in His word, and above all things—love!

Pray

Lord Jesus, thank you that we do not have to wait for your judgment or your love. Please judge me now. I do not want to wait. Wash me with a spirit of judgment and burning. Let me become a pure bride on fire.

Study Guide: page 226

23 | Redeeming the Bride

1 Timothy 1:5 (NASB)
"But the goal of our instruction is love from a pure heart and a good conscience and a sincere faith."

It is a great honour to be called to teach others and reopen the well of God's love in people's hearts. Yet, as teachers, we need to be aware that the enemy will often tempt us to drift into either legalism or license, hoping to divert our message away from the gospel of love. We therefore need to keep returning to the goal of our instruction: love, love, love!

A Word to Teachers

Deuteronomy 13:1-4
"If a prophet or a dreamer of dreams arises among you and gives you a sign or a wonder, and the sign or wonder that he tells you comes to pass, and if he says, 'Let us go after other gods,' which you have not known, 'and let us serve them,' you shall not listen to the words of that prophet or that dreamer of dreams. For the LORD your God is testing you, to know whether you love the LORD your God with all your heart and with all your soul. You shall walk after the LORD your God and fear him and keep his commandments and obey his voice, and you shall serve him and hold fast to [live in unity with] him."

1 John 4:1
Beloved, do not believe every spirit, but test the spirits to see whether they are from God, for many false prophets have gone out into the world.

It is sobering to think that signs and wonders will be performed by people who are preaching a false gospel of a different Jesus. False theology is one of the enemy's greatest weapons against us, and so John calls us to test the spirit behind every teaching, dream or vision. As we see here, the fulfilment of signs and wonders is no indication at all that a teaching is from God.[1] We test a teaching by Scripture's standard of love. Does the teaching put the first command in first place? Does it affirm God's design of love, intimacy and unity with Him?

> **Galatians 1:6-7**
> I am astonished that you are so quickly deserting him who called you in the grace of Christ and are turning to a different gospel— not that there is another one, but there are some who trouble you and want to distort the gospel of Christ.

Paul sought to prepare believers as a bride for Christ, establishing them in the simplicity of and purity of devotion to Christ. But after Paul left, other teachers came in who did not share the same vision. Some sought to lead the people into legalism, others into license. Many drew people to depend on them and their ministry. What these "leaders" failed to realise is that in the spiritual realm, dependency is intimacy.[2] By leading people to depend on them, these teachers were becoming intimate with the bride and defiling her. Instead of preparing the bride for Jesus, they were grooming the bride for themselves.

There is only one ultimate call for all teachers: prepare the bride for Jesus! Regardless of whether a teacher has a good reputation or successful ministry in the Christian world, if their teaching diverts people away from a wholehearted love for God then they will have to answer to God. Imagine being such a teacher! Imagine finally entering into heaven and hearing the Father say, "I called you to prepare a bride for My Son. Where is she?"[3]

Caught in the Drift

James 3:1

Not many of you should become teachers, my brothers, for you know
that we who teach will be judged with greater strictness.

The call to prepare the bride is the reason why teachers can expect a stricter
judgment. Depending on what is taught, teachers can directly release or stem
the flow of the Father's love to Jesus. If they ignore the first command and
fail to empower people to become the bride of Christ, then they deny Jesus a
measure of the love He died for. This means that their teaching has eternal
consequences felt by Jesus Christ Himself. It is therefore essential that we all
get our theology right and avoid even the slightest hint of legalism or license.
If we are teachers, we are in a place of great power and privilege—one that
comes with a tremendous responsibility to be found faithful. We simply must
align all our teaching to the standard of love and truth.

I learned the bitter consequences of not testing teaching soon after I was
married to Jesus. I taught about the bride in a church group, but it did not fit
with the pastors' theology and they were keen for me to leave. I found a small
church and at first it was amazing. There was a tangible sense of life and joy
every time we met. We were all growing together in the love of God. Over
time however, a spirit of legalism crept into the fellowship. It was subtle at
first; a gradual increase of manipulation and a shift of focus away from love.
The leadership wanted to impact the city and so they started teaching that if
we gave more money we would be blessed by God. Yet they also implied that
those who did not give would be cursed by God. Everyone was called to pray
harder and longer for breakthrough. We were all pressured to pray for at
least an hour of a 24-hour schedule of prayer. Slowly but surely, we drifted
into legalism and became subject to a spirit of fear and control.

I was leading the music team at the time. One Sunday morning, the pastor
came to me and instructed me to sing a certain set of songs.

"Do these songs first and then do that one, because the presence of God
comes with that song," he instructed. I did as I was asked and began to lead

the people in worship. During the singing, the Lord opened my eyes to see in the spirit. Outside the back doors of the church I saw the throne-room of heaven, surrounded in light. Jesus and the Father were there. I watched as our worship ascended towards them. Then a demon appeared between us and the throne-room, and it started receiving the worship that we intended for God. I could hardly believe my eyes.

"What's going on?!" I asked. The Spirit responded.

"When you use worship to manipulate me or to invoke my presence, you are not worshipping me at all. You are worshipping a demon of works," God replied. He was looking past the music to our heart. It was true. We were using our songs to try and earn the blessing of God's presence rather than simply bring a blessing to Him. There was no humility in our singing. We were not ministering to Jesus, nor were we worshipping in spirit or truth. It was a musical fantasy and we were calling it worship. And I was leading it.

I was stunned. Here I was, the bride of Christ, leading God's people in worship to a religious demon. *How did I get here?* Even though I saw what was happening, I was too afraid to stop. I told myself that God had shown me the vision so I could bind the demon and release true worship to God. But I was lying to myself to cover over my fear. A spirit of legalism was ruling over the church, and at that moment, it was ruling over me.

Over the following weeks, God called me to leave the fellowship. *Come out from there and touch no unclean thing!* Even though God confirmed His word, the yoke of legalism was heavy and enslaving. My closest friends wanted to stay and encouraged me to keep going. I pretended that maybe things would change. It took some months, but I finally found the strength to obey God's voice. I left, spiritually shattered. I felt used, abused, and unclean. Most of all, I missed the intimacy and love I used to enjoy with Jesus. I so deeply missed Him.

I woke up one morning with my heart aching for Jesus. I spent some time reading over some testimonies of people who were involved in the Wesleyan revival of the 1700's. This was a revival that was fuelled by the first command. One quote stood out to me, the source of which I have since forgotten:

"For ten years now, I have walked under the cloudless skies of the Sun of Righteousness."

Ten years in the unbroken presence of God. *Ten years.* It made my heart ache even more. I so wanted the presence of God and to share my Father's love for Jesus. I so wanted the Son to shine His light upon me. I tried to worship but I felt numb. I could not sense anything of the presence of God. Instead, there was just a void in the spirit.

"Lord, I just want to worship you." I was still trying to understand what was happening. God's response was firm and clear: "Do not worship me."

I thought I must be mishearing God or maybe I was hearing the voice of the enemy. After all, this is what we do. God is God, and we are His creation. We are called to worship Him. So I tried to start worshipping again, and again His voice came clearly.

"Do not worship me. Let's go for a walk."

I went outside and began to walk up the street. I was on a hill and could see out over the whole city, which was covered in a dense fog. I looked directly at the sun. It was like a dim light, barely visible behind the cloud. I knew that the sky was a picture of my heart. The light could hardly be seen.

"You're showing me my heart, aren't you?" I said to God.

"Yes. You have fallen into prostitution," He replied. The voice of God was compassionate and yet heart-breaking. I had returned to the old husband of legalism. I had spent so long preparing as a bride and devoted my life to loving Jesus, only to fall into spiritual prostitution within months.

I cried.

"Oh God, I am so, so sorry! Forgive me! Please forgive me," was all I could say.

"I have made you holy for my glory," the Lord responded. With those words, God washed away all my guilt, broke the power of legalism, and restored me back to my purity as the bride of Christ. It all happened in an instant. The restoration of my shattered heart was so quick that a part of me was not sure it was real. So I asked God to confirm that I was truly restored.

"Lord, if this is true, and you really have cleansed my heart from my prostitution, would you please clear the sky by the time I get home?" I asked. He did not respond, but we continued walking together for another ten or fifteen minutes. I arrived back home and looked up at the sky. All the clouds were gone, and the entire sky was a brilliant blue. I looked out over the city, as it basked in the blazing sunlight. It felt like a new day had begun, and it was beautiful.

Restoring Love

Hosea 3:1

And the LORD said to me, "Go again, love a woman who is loved by another man and is an adulteress, even as the LORD loves the children of Israel, though they turn to other gods and love cakes of raisins."

Jesus is compassionate and loving beyond words. When He takes you as His bride, walk in faithfulness. Guard your heart against every form of legalism and license, both of which are spiritual prostitution. Guard your heart at all cost! Love always. Hear His voice. Act in union with Him.

But know that if you do fall, Jesus will be there to pick you up. Like Hosea or Boaz, Jesus is our Bridegroom *and* our Redeemer. So if you carelessly step outside your unity with Christ and are deceived by sin, simply repent and return to your First Love. Know that His arms are always open and be quick to return to His embrace. Like Hosea, Jesus will heal you, restore you and raise you up, and you will again be one with the eternal Son of Love.

Pray

Lord Jesus, I know my call is to be faithful. But I cannot do it alone. I need you. Please keep me from all prostitution. Please help me to test the teaching that I hear and nourish me with teaching that does not distract me from loving you. And please help me to prepare your bride in humility and selfless love.

24 | Living in Love

There is no higher call than that of becoming the bride of Christ and being one spirit with Jesus for all eternity. Yet like natural marriage, it is only when we first get married that we realise we have a lifetime of learning, growth and change before us. Being married to Jesus does not mean that we have reached the perfection of our lives. Far from it! Rather, it simply means that we have entered into a new depth of relationship with Jesus, and like every relationship, we begin in a place of infancy.

When Israel arrived in the Promised Land, there were still nations to conquer and cities to take, and our marriage to Jesus is the same. Our minds still need to be renewed to align more with His truth. We still need to grow in love and all its many expressions. Our understanding needs to increase as well as our clarity. We will still make mistakes, we may hurt people, and we may still stumble on occasion. But we need to remember, the goal of our marriage is not perfect behaviour, but perfect love. And if the love of the Father is flowing through us to Jesus, it is perfect in any measure, be it small or great.

> **Proverbs 4:18**
> The path of the righteous is like the first gleam of dawn, shining brighter and brighter until midday.

We should not be discouraged if we feel like our capacity for love is small at first. Jesus treasures the love of the Father beyond all expression, even in its smallest measure. In this respect, the love and intimacy we first experience in marriage can be likened to the radiance of the sun. There is incredible beauty on display with the sunrise. Yet the sun at its rising looks so different to the sun at midday. Even with the protection of the sky, when the sun is shining at its full strength, its brilliance is overwhelming.

Like the sun, every stage of our marriage to Jesus has its own beauty. Jesus is not disappointed that the sunrise does not give the same warmth as the noonday sun, and neither is He disappointed that our love at first may not be as intense as we would like. He simply looks at His bride and enjoys her beauty, knowing that she will grow ever stronger and shine ever brighter.

Growing up into Christ

Ephesians 4:15-16

Rather, speaking the truth in love, we are to grow up in every way into [*eis*] him who is the head, into [*eis*] Christ, from whom the whole body, joined and held together by every joint with which it is equipped, when each part is working properly, makes the body grow so that it builds itself up in love.

As we learned earlier, the word translated as *into* is the Greek word *eis* meaning "into; a motion into union."[1] It has the sense of an active movement that leads to a union.

This passage calls us "to grow up in every way into Jesus." This is an invitation to constantly explore the different ways that we can build our unity with Jesus. For example, we build our unity of heart through sacrificial worship and practical love. We build our unity of nature as we partake of Christ's living bread and exchange our nature for His. We increase our unity of spirit by drinking the wine of the new covenant, the blood of Christ, and being filled again with the life of His Spirit. We increase our unity of will through prayer as we exchange our desires with His and then act with Him. We deepen our unity of mind as we take time to listen for His voice and to be renewed by His word. We increase our unity of emotion as we abide in the secret place and behold His beauty.

Beyond the spiritual disciplines, every situation we encounter in life, whether joyful or painful, gives us an opportunity to grow into Jesus and increase our love for Him. In fact, the greatest potential for growth is often found in the hardest trials.

Psalm 23:1-4

The LORD is my shepherd; I shall not want.

He makes me lie down in green pastures.

He leads me beside still waters.

He restores my soul.

He leads me in paths of righteousness for his name's sake.

Even though I walk through the valley of the shadow of death,

I will fear no evil, for you are with me;

your rod and your staff, they comfort me.

In Psalm 23, we can see the stretch-and-grow process of love. Jesus as our Shepherd-King loves us by leading us to green pastures to give us times of refreshing and restoration. Yet He also loves us by leading us into the valley of the shadow of death. He knows that the valley is the best place to enlarge our hearts for love. Jesus promises that He will never leave us, but He will let us go through hard and even painful times. We may encounter great loss or even tragedy. During these times, the enemy will use offence or bitterness or unforgiveness to tempt us to stop loving. But if we can find the grace in our temporal trials to keep choosing love, God will stretch our hearts and we will reap the reward of a greater capacity for loving Jesus. And this is the glory that will remain with us for all eternity.

Intimacy

Psalm 139:17-18 (The Discovery Bible)

How <u>precious</u>•⁻ also are Your thoughts to <u>me</u>, O God!

How vast•⁻ is the sum of them!

If I should count them, they would <u>outnumber the sand.</u>

When I ⌐awake,•⁻ I am still with You.

In our natural marriages, our unity grows as we share our hearts and minds with one another. It is the same in the spirit. Sharing the thoughts of God is an ongoing key to building our intimacy and unity with Jesus. In these verses, David communicates a beautiful truth about the thoughts of God, hidden just below the surface of the words.

The word translated as *thoughts* is the Hebrew word *rea,* which comes from the root word (also *rea*) meaning *friendship.* It is not limited to logical thought but encompasses every expression of affection. When God shares His *rea* with us, it can often simply be a feeling, impression or intuition. At times we may receive some understanding apart from words, like a dawning revelation. His voice may come to us as a dream or vision, or He may speak to us in a flow of unexpected, articulated thought. Regardless of how God speaks, every word is powerful. Every word is an expression of affection, filled with spirit and life.

In this passage, the words which are marked with the •- symbol are written in what is called the *Hebrew perfect aspect.*[2] The Hebrew perfect describes a completed action that sets the platform for something else to happen. When the Hebrew perfect is found in groups, each perfect word builds on the one before like stairs on a staircase. This creates a crescendo effect within the text—a growing intensity that builds up to a particular outcome.

How precious•- are your thoughts to me, O God

Like David, if we personally treasure the thoughts and affections of God, treating them as immensely precious in our lives, we create a platform in our hearts for something to happen.

How vast•- is the sum of them

When we appreciate that God is constantly wanting to share His affections with us, we add to that platform and set the stage for something else to follow.

When I awake•-

This awakening is not speaking simply of physically waking up in the morning, but rather it is speaking of a spiritual awakening in the life of the believer.[3] It is an awakening of the heart that comes from treasuring the affections of God, which itself sets a platform for experiencing more of God's presence in our lives: *I am still with You.*

The message of this passage is simple and yet profound. We cannot begin to comprehend the incredible depths of God's love towards us. He is always thinking about us and He always wants to share His affections with us. If we would learn to recognise His voice; if we would treasure His thoughts; if we would start to live in this flow of intimate affection, we would find our hearts awakened and aware of the presence of Jesus within us. And it would change our lives forever.

No Longer I

1 Corinthians 6:17
But he who is joined to the Lord becomes one spirit with him.

God knows that it takes time to come to truly believe that Jesus lives within us. It requires a whole new way of thinking, which is why the Holy Spirit wants to renew our minds with His affections. Every thought that the Spirit of God shares with us helps us to become more aware that Jesus is with us, He loves us, and we are one with Him.

We can think of our unity with Jesus in the sense of a shared life. When we get married in the natural realm, we bring an end to our life as a single person and we start to share our spaces of life with our spouse. We share our home, our food, our income, our time, our bodies, our minds, and our very hearts with each other. Though we are one with our spouse, we do not change into them. Instead, we create a unique unity together as a couple and this leaves us permanently changed.

In the same way, when we come into marriage to Jesus, our lives become a shared space with Him. Our minds become a shared space as Jesus shares His thoughts with us and we share ours with Him.[4] Our hearts become a shared space as Jesus shares His heart with us and we share ours with Him. The more we share the heart and mind of Christ, the more His love changes the way we think, how we feel, and how we live.

Galatians 2:20

I have been crucified with Christ. It is no longer I who live, but Christ who lives in me. And the life I now live in the flesh I live by faith in the Son of God, who loved me and gave himself for me.

When we get married in the natural realm, we bring an end to our life as a single person and it is no longer I that live—it is now *We*. For example, before I married Melanie, I only needed to think about myself. When we got married, that had to change. I could no longer just think of myself when acting or making decisions. Instead, I had to learn how to think in a way that honoured Melanie. The same is true in our relationship with Jesus. When our thoughts start with *I*, we are thinking of Jesus *and* me rather than Jesus *in* me. If we are to honour our unity with Jesus, we need to train our minds to start thinking *We*.

***

"I can't do this." The workload before me seemed overwhelming and inescapable, so I shared my thoughts with God, "I can't do this."

"What do you mean 'I'?" the Spirit of God replied. "When we became one, you gave up your right to start any inner thought with the word 'I'. Try again."

"Fine. We ca…" I desperately wanted to say *"can't"*, but I could not do it. I could not deliberately lie to God. The Spirit of Jesus was compelling me to accept the truth and to voice it in my thoughts. I gave in.

"OK. We can do this. So where do we start?"

Once I had broken the lie and accepted the truth, I felt a new sense of empowerment. Jesus and I were working together. We were one. The work I thought would take six months to complete was almost finished in just three weeks. I realised that I had over-estimated the volume of work, but I also found that God's grace was present to work hard and fruitfully.

It is important to note that when we start to think *We*, we are in no way making ourselves equal with God or beginning to think of ourselves as Jesus.

We are not Jesus and we never will be Jesus. God alone is God. We can see this principle in natural marriage. I am married to my wife Melanie, but I am not my wife. We share our lives, our love, our visions, dreams, and our hearts with each other. We are one flesh, but I am not Melanie and she is not me. So it is with our marriage to Jesus. Though we have a new identity in unity with Jesus, we still retain our own unique personality. In our conversations with people we still say *"I"* because outwardly we are still individual people with an individual identity. But inwardly, we need to learn to think *We* and account for our unity with Jesus. This is an ongoing process of retraining and renewing the mind. If we persist in trusting God to change the way we think, we will find whole new realms of faith and love open up to us. We will begin to truly believe that all things are possible because we are in Christ Jesus and He is in us. It is no longer I who lives, but Christ who lives in me: *We.*

Pray

Jesus, I love to be one with you. Thank you for calling me to be your bride. The thought of never being alone but living in union with you for the rest of my life is awesome beyond words. Please open my eyes to see all your affections. Please let me feel your love as it flows through me. Help me to honour our union and to learn to think "We."

25 | Bride and Glory

When we live in unity with the Spirit, we can share the nature of God in our relationships. For example, if we are parents, we can share the Father's heart and parent our children in unity with Him. As the Father's wisdom and love flow through us, our children can discover what God is like through us. In the same way, in our friendships, we can share the heart of Christ so that we can love our friends the way Jesus loves His friends. We can also share Jesus's love for our spouse so that our marriages on earth reflect the glory of our heavenly marriage. So what is the heart of Christ for His bride like?

Goodness and Glory

Ezekiel 16:12-14

And I put a ring on your nose and earrings in your ears and a beautiful crown on your head. Thus you were adorned with gold and silver, and your clothing was of fine linen and silk and embroidered cloth. You ate fine flour and honey and oil. You grew exceedingly beautiful and advanced to royalty. And your renown went forth among the nations because of your beauty, for it was perfect through the splendour that I had bestowed on you, declares the LORD God.

Jeremiah 33:9

"And this city shall be to me a name of joy, a praise and a glory before all the nations of the earth who shall hear of all the good that I do for them. They shall fear and tremble because of all the good and all the prosperity I provide for it." [1]

The heart of Christ is to adorn His bride and make her exceedingly beautiful and extravagantly blessed. Jesus wants His bride to radiate His glory by being the living proof of His goodness on the earth. Jesus receives glory when we selflessly love others. He receives glory when we spread His joy in the world. Whenever we share His wisdom, peace, kindness or hope with others, Jesus receives all the glory. It is God's desire to pour out so much of His goodness and love through us that people in the world are literally left in awe. This is the beauty and glory of Christ on display in His bride.

This is true in the spiritual realm, but can this principle of glory also apply in our natural marriages?

The Living Glory

Genesis 5:1b-2
When God created man, he made him in the likeness of God. Male and female he created them, and he blessed them and named them Man when they were created.

In the beginning, God created men and women in His likeness, and together He called them *Man*. In Christ, there is neither male nor female, and He does not value one higher than the other. We can see our equality before God in the greatest command—there are no separate versions of the command for men and women. We are all called to live in covenant love and unity with Jesus, and this gives us all equal and immeasurable value before God.

1 Corinthians 11:3,7
But I want you to understand that the head of every man is Christ, the head of a wife is her husband, and the head of Christ is God...For a man ought not to cover his head, since he is the image and glory of God, but woman is the glory of man.

In terms of the marriage relationship, God gives woman to man in the same way that He gives us as a bride to Christ. His design for marriage is that the wife would be the living expression of the husband's glory, because she is the primary receiver of her husband's love. The more love she receives, the more beautiful she becomes, and the greater glory she gives to her husband. There is no question or threat of inequality in this. It is all about love.

Ephesians 5:18-27

And do not get drunk with wine, for that is debauchery, but be filled with the Spirit, addressing one another in psalms and hymns and spiritual songs, singing and making melody to the Lord with your heart, giving thanks always and for everything to God the Father in the name of our Lord Jesus Christ, submitting to one another out of reverence for Christ. Wives submit to your own husbands, as to the Lord. For the husband is the head of the wife even as Christ is the head of the church, his body, and is himself its Saviour. Now as the church submits to Christ, so also wives should submit in everything to their husbands.

Husbands, love your wives, as Christ loved the church and gave himself up for her, that he might sanctify her, having cleansed her by the washing of water with the word, so that he might present the church to himself in splendour, without spot or wrinkle or any such thing, that she might be holy and without blemish.

"For the husband is the head of the wife even as Christ is the head of the church." If we are married, as the husband, we are the head of our wife. For too long people have focused on headship as the right of the man to lead, dictate to, or even dominate his wife. But Scripture says that the Father is the head of Jesus.[2] This is not a headship of control, dominance or superiority, but one of extravagant love. It is like the head of a river—a source and spring that flows with love, goodness, unity and joy. This is the true headship that Jesus wants to release through husbands.

"Husbands, love your wives, as Christ loved the church." At first glance, this verse might seem to set an impossibly high standard for husbands to keep. However, we need to know that **only Jesus can love like Jesus**. When Scripture calls us to love like Jesus, it is calling us to let Jesus love our wives through us. Understanding this brings instant hope to our marriages. As

husbands, we do not ever have to pretend or try to fabricate love. We simply need to become channels of God's love for our wives.

"Lord, I don't love my wife, and I don't love you…" Melanie and I were less than six months into our marriage when I started feeling empty. In the beginning, it was easy to be carried along by feelings. When the feelings faded, I felt like I had to force myself to love. Yet all my striving left me in an emotional void that I felt helpless to fill. On that day I stopped trying to love. Instead, I asked God to share His love with me.

"I don't love my wife, and I don't love you…but I want to. Can you help me to love?" This was a prayer that Jesus was quick to answer.

As our head and source of love, Jesus longs to love our wives through us. But because His love is a gift that we can only receive by faith, Jesus has to wait for us to stop striving before He can release His love. As we surrender to His headship, we uncover the wells of His grace and start to experience His love for our wives. And what is that love like? It is a selfless, relentless, unbreakable, undistracted and utterly extravagant love.

As Melanie and I grew in love, the Lord took us into a season where each day we both prayed, "Lord, how do you want to love Melanie/Geoff through me today?" Each time we prayed, God showed us a unique expression of love for that day. The more we looked to God to be the source of love in our marriage, the more love He shared with us. During this time, God gave me a promise to help set me free to love Melanie extravagantly.

"I want you to love Melanie as I love the church—without limit. To help you do this, feel free to spend as much time and as much money on Melanie as you like, and I will make it up. I will replace the money, and I will replace the time by enabling you to achieve more in less time," God said. I knew God was good, but this was hard to believe. We have always depended on God to provide for us and so have felt that to honour God's provision, we needed to be careful with how we spend His money. But now He was telling me to be completely free to invest His money in love?! Could God be this good? Surely there must be some reasonable limits to love?

After He said this, I felt that Jesus wanted to buy Melanie some flowers. So for the first time in many years, I bought her flowers. The next day I took her out to a café.

"Lord, I have spent $50 on Melanie so far this week," I said, just to remind Him of His promise.

"And what did I give you in the weekend?" He replied, and I remembered the gift a friend gave me.

"Oh. A $50 voucher." God had kept His promise in advance and His call remained firm: *Love extravagantly.*

This promise was not an open invitation for me to fill Melanie's life with expensive possessions or to be wasteful with our time or money. Rather, it was an invitation to fully love Melanie *with* the Spirit of Jesus, without worrying about the cost of time or money. It was a promise that put my marriage into perspective. Our marriage is incredibly important to God. Why? Because ultimately our marriage is a channel of love between the Father and Son. The love that the Father pours out through me to Melanie is not only received by her, but it is also felt by the Spirit of Jesus within her. And the love for me that the Father shares with Melanie is ultimately received by the Spirit of Jesus within me. The more we love God, the more we love each other, the more we love God.

This flow of love is at the foundation of all our relationships with other believers, but it is uniquely special within marriage. Marriage is based on an exclusive covenant of love, which raises this relationship above all others. This means that the second most important command—to love others—begins with our marriages. This is our first place of obedience. For if we cannot share God's love for our spouse, how can we share His love for anyone else? If Jesus is our first love spiritually, how can our spouse be anything but our first love in the natural?

Humility and Love

Ephesians 4:1-3

I therefore, a prisoner for the Lord, urge you to walk in a manner worthy of the calling to which you have been called, with all humility and gentleness, with patience, bearing with one another in love, eager to maintain the unity of the Spirit in the bond of peace.

In Chapter 11 we learned how God humbles Himself to love us. Even though He longs to consume our entire lives with His love and blessings, Jesus humbles Himself to only give us as much as we are willing to receive. Though His heart is continually bursting with love, Jesus does not force the fullness of His love upon us. Instead, He patiently waits for us to grow in our capacity to receive love.

As husbands, we need to apply this principle of humility in our marriages. There will come times when we need to humble ourselves to love our wife at a level she can receive. There may be days when we feel full of sexual desire, but if we listen to the Spirit, we may feel prompted to restrain our desire and instead cook dinner or simply take time to listen to our wife. The key is to love with the Spirit of Jesus. The way He leads us in love may change on different days or seasons, but one thing will always be true: His love will only ever flow through humility.

Guarding the Glory

Our wives are our glory, and there can be times when we need to guard our glory, even from ourselves. I saw this when Melanie and I met with a young couple for breakfast. They arrived a few minutes late.

"Hey, I'm sorry we're late. It's her fault," the husband said. He blamed his wife in order to protect his own pride, but in doing so he gave away her glory. Without realising it, he created a small crack in their foundation of love.

Imagine if the new husband had humbled himself and hidden his wife's fault? We would never have known, and by protecting her from blame, he would have quietly blessed her in the presence of others. She would have become more beautiful and his glory would have increased.[3]

Our words are powerful. We must *never* speak against our spouse. We must *never* belittle, mock, embarrass, or blame them in front of others. To do so is to sow division within our marriage. Marriage is a commitment to unity. This means sharing each other's success and failure as if they were our own.

To preserve the unity, we need to identify and repent of all pride. Pride always blames others and seeks to maintain its own reputation. Pride always wants to be right at the other person's expense. Pride is quick to discover the faults in others and it keeps a record of all wrongs for future use. In every way, pride sacrifices glory.

Love is the opposite. It flows through humility and covers over sin. It always lifts up, beautifies and unites. Love preserves unity at its own expense. It does not mind appearing broken or foolish and it accepts correction with grace. Love does not fight for its reputation. Love keeps no record of wrongs and nor does it ever seek to lay blame. In every way, love brings forth glory. This is the love that God has for us and it is the kind of love that He wants for our marriages. This is a love worth sharing.

Pray

Lord, thank you for your design for marriage. Thank you that you want our relationships to be made glorious through your selfless love. Please let your love flow through me in extravagance, grace and beauty.

Please read the Study Guide on page 229 to find more prayers suited to different situations such as married, single, husband, or wife.

26 | Aligned to Design

The highest manifestation of God's glory is not in His power flowing through signs, wonders, or miracles; it is in His love flowing through looks, words, and actions.[1] So if we want to bring God the greatest glory through our marriages, then we need to pursue the greatest love possible.

True love is always selfless and so the opposite of love is not hate but selfishness. For this reason, the enemy will continually try to destroy our marriage love through selfishness. *Do what is best for you. Put your needs first. Give, but use it as leverage for taking later. Keep score. Win.*[2]

The reality is that we cannot choose love and selfishness. If we choose love, we will experience the fruit of joy, freedom and unity in our marriage. If we choose selfishness, our marriage will become a source of competition, conflict, division, frustration, and even pain. We already make this choice between love and selfishness subconsciously every day. But now is the time to make a conscious decision to choose selfless love.

Ephesians 5:18-24[3]

And do not get drunk with wine, for that is debauchery, but be filled with the Spirit, addressing one another in psalms and hymns and spiritual songs, singing and making melody to the Lord with your heart, giving thanks always and for everything to God the Father in the name of our Lord Jesus Christ, submitting to one another out of reverence for Christ, wives to your own husbands, as to the Lord. For the husband is the head of the wife even as Christ is the head of the church, his body, and is himself its Saviour. Now as the church submits to Christ, so also wives should submit in everything to their husbands.

Full Submission

Submit/Be subject: *hypotássō*

From 5259/hypó, "under" and 5021/tássō, "arrange"; – properly, "under God's arrangement," i.e. submitting to the Lord (His plan).

"...submitting to one another out of reverence for Christ..." Returning to this passage, we find that Scripture calls us to submit to one another as a way of revering Christ in one another. The word *submit* here is the Greek word *hypotasso*, which means to put under God's arrangement. If we are to honour Jesus, we need to arrange our relationships according to His design. This applies to all our relationships and especially to our marriages.

God's design is for husbands to be a channel of Jesus' love for their wives. Wives are called to submit to that design and allow their husbands to love them with the love of Christ. It is a sad reality that many women have experienced trauma or pain in their past that affects their ability to receive genuine love. If you are carrying hurt from your past, then know that God wants to fully heal your heart and remove every resistance to love. If you are willing to forgive and to be healed, He will do whatever it takes to make you whole and restore your capacity for love.

"...wives to your own husbands, as to the Lord." Scripture calls wives to submit to their husbands, *as to the Lord.* This does not mean that a wife should treat her husband as if he was God. Rather, wives need to submit to their husbands for the same reasons we submit to God.

We submit to the Lord in order to align our lives with His design. The same is true for our marriages. Wives are called to align with God's design for love, intimacy and unity within their marriages. This design provides no room for selfishness. This means that while wives are called to submit to their husband's love, they are equally called to resist their husband's selfishness. Light cannot submit to darkness, nor spirit to flesh, and so wives are not called to submit to their husband's selfish nature *in any way.* To do so would be to fail to arrange the marriage according to God's design.

Submission does not always mean obedience. They are different words in both Greek and English for a reason. Scripture calls wives to submit to their husbands, but it never requires unquestioning obedience in marriage. For wives, if your husband wanted to prostitute you, would it please God for you to obey your husband and become a prostitute? No! Would submitting to your husband's abuse give God glory? No! Would your obedience help to bring the marriage into God's design? No! This principle may seem obvious when applied to prostitution, but would it be so clear if the husband's desire was less extreme, but still selfish, abusive or degrading? Is it acceptable to submit to a mild form of abuse?

Galatians 6:8
For the one who sows to his own flesh will from the flesh reap corruption, but the one who sows to the Spirit will from the Spirit reap eternal life.

Regardless of the level of selfishness, any agreement with the flesh will reap corruption. For example, many people believe that sexual desire and lust are the same thing. They believe that lust outside marriage is sin, but within marriage, lust is no longer lust, rather it is just sexual passion. The reality is that marriage does not sanctify lust at all. Lust is a powerful expression of selfishness. It always takes. Lust makes us want to use someone's body for our own pleasure. It is never about selfless love or giving pleasure to the other person. And because it is rooted in selfishness, lust can never be satisfied. It always wants more and will eventually look outside the marriage to fulfil its endless cravings.

If wives submit to their husbands' lust, then they will reap corruption from the flesh. If they sacrifice their dignity and reduce themselves to be objects for their husbands' pleasure, both husband and wife will reap the fruit of emptiness and unfulfillment. Neither husband nor wife can afford to submit to the selfish nature. This only defiles the design of God for their marriage and forfeits His glory. There is a much better way.

A Fit Helper

Genesis 2:18

Then the LORD God said, "It is not good that the man should be alone; I will make him a helper fit for him."

Fit Helper: *neged-ezer*

"According to what is in front of – corresponding to…A help corresponding to him i.e. equal and adequate to himself."[4]

God gave Eve to Adam as a *neged-ezer*. The Hebrew word *ezer* means *helper* and is often used in a military context, speaking of a stronger military force coming to the aid of the weaker. Most often in Scripture it is used to speak of God as a helper to His people.[5] God gave Eve to Adam, not as a superior force, but as a helper equal to her husband.

God brings men and women together in marriage with different but equally valuable roles. Men are called to release the love of Christ into their wives as a head-spring of goodness. Women are called to be the glory of their husbands and helpers who fight for God's design. In her healed and whole state, every wife has this ability.

One of the most powerful statements that my wife Melanie ever said to me was this: *"You must improve."* I was being lazy around the home, and she was having to do extra work to make up for my laziness. I knew I was being lazy. She knew it. But nothing changed until she challenged me about it.

This was just a small example of a much bigger picture. As a *neged-ezer*, the wife needs to fight to bring her husband into his true identity. This starts with having a clear vision of who God has created her husband to be. Once she has a vision for her first-command husband, she can believe for him, even before he starts to believe for himself. She can release the full force of her anointing to bring her husband higher. *You can do better than this. God did not create you to live at this level. You are better and you must improve. Don't give in to the anger or lust or pride. We'll fight it together. I love you with all my heart, and I'll die fighting for the true you.*

The Power of the Cross

Scripture paints the flesh or old-man as the deadliest threat to our new identity in Christ. This is why wives must not submit to the flesh of their husbands. To tolerate your husband's pride or lust or anger is to deny his true identity. He needs you to resist his flesh and believe for him to become his true self. He needs you to call him higher. This is your love.

It is important to understand that the selfish nature is far too strong to be overcome simply by good intentions or sheer willpower. Therefore, both husbands and wives need to avoid putting pressure on each other to change. Instead, we need to point one another to the only power that can truly conquer selfishness: the cross.

Through the cross, Jesus has released the power of His blood to take away our sin *and the selfish nature at the root of all sin*. For this reason, Scripture speaks of the cross as the knife that circumcises the heart.[6] If we have the faith, God will use the cross to cut the selfishness out of our hearts so that we can selflessly love. But this is not an experience we can enter into casually. Wholehearted love is only found by those who seek it with their whole hearts. So we must be intentional. We must turn against our own selfishness and put the first command in first place in our marriages. When we surrender to the call of love, we can be sure that God will be faithful to keep His promise and circumcise our hearts. He wants this more than us and He will do everything in His power to make it a reality. We simply need to say *Yes*.

Overcoming the Strongholds

In the book *First Love,* we look at how the lies we believe can bring us into agreement with demonic spirits. This gives them permission to affect the way we think, feel and act. Their work in our marriages can often be subtle and hard to discern, but if we let the Holy Spirit expose these agreements, we can end the influence of those spirits in our marriages. This became crystal clear to me in the late hours of one night.

I was having trouble sleeping, so I went to the lounge to pray. We have a decal of the first command on our lounge wall. I focused on it and prayed.

"God, I have to love you with all my heart and soul. Please Lord. This is who I am. I have to love you," I prayed and the Spirit of God responded quite unexpectedly.

"You need to repent of rejection," He spoke in a clear thought. I did not fully understand why, but I proceeded to pray.

"Father, I am sorry for agreeing with rejection. I am sorry for rejecting others. I repent. I renounce all rejection and I reject it from my life. I break every agreement with rejection and cancel its permission to operate in my life."

I was wondering why I would need to repent from rejection rather than be healed from it. I felt God speak and give me some understanding.

"Rejection came down through your family bloodline from your grandfather…" I knew my grandfather was forced out of home and country at the age of 16, and never saw or talked to his family again.

"…He passed it on to your father, who then passed it on to you."

"But Lord, surely that is something to be healed from rather than to repent of?"

"When you were first rejected by your father, you accepted that rejection. You agreed with it and that gave permission to a spirit of rejection to be on your life. People would like you and like your message, but they would reject you because of that spirit on your life. Repentance breaks the permission that allows that spirit to remain and expels it from your life."

It all made sense. All through my life, and even in my marriage, that spirit had been working to bring different forms of rejection. I went back to bed with a new sense of peace, and freedom. To my surprise, I found Melanie awake. Though I thought she had been sleeping, God had woken her to also deal with a spirit of rejection. While God was talking to me in the lounge, He was speaking with Melanie in the bedroom, setting us both free at the same time.

She told me later what God had said to her.

"He spoke so clearly, saying, 'You must choose between control and love. You have been rejecting the safe leadership of your husband and your rebellion is as the sin of witchcraft.'" God was speaking the truth in love and exposing the spiritual dynamics that were undermining our marriage. The same spirit of rejection that I carried in my life had also gained an agreement with Melanie. We both repented. God set us free together so that rejection could no longer have any hold in our marriage.

Whenever we accept any compromise with the enemy such as control or fear or rejection, we invite demonic spirits into our marriages to steal our love, kill our intimacy, and destroy our glory. This direct connection with the enemy is why such compromises are like practicing witchcraft in the eyes of God. In order to align our marriages with God's design, both husbands and wives need to war against every temptation to control, manipulate, disrespect or reject each other. Every agreement with the enemy must be broken and replaced with a new agreement with God. By choosing selfless love, humility, intimacy, joy and unity in our marriages, we give the Holy Spirit permission to transform our marriages and bring them into His design. And we can be certain that He will do it. It is God's desire is to turn our marriages into living reflections of the love of our Bridegroom for His bride. He is only waiting for our agreement.

Pray

Father, thank you for the call to align all my relationships with your design. Please help me to do this. Let your love and blessing flow in every relationship.

If you would like to start dealing with some strongholds, please read the Study Guide for this chapter on page 235.

27 | To Love and Obey

Matthew 6:9-10
"Pray then like this:
'Our Father in heaven,
    hallowed be your name.
Your kingdom come,
    your will be done,
    on earth as it is in heaven.'"

Here Jesus shows us how to pray. We start by declaring our relationship to God: He is our Father and we are His children. We then focus on the name of our Father. As we learned earlier, the name of God represents His nature of infinite love, extreme goodness, and intense holiness. We revere His name as we behold the beauty of His nature.[1] When we become confident in the nature of our Father, we can then pray with passion that His kingdom would come and His will would be done in our lives on earth, as it is in heaven.[2]

This is an awesome prayer, but we need to ask: What is the cost of praying this? Can we truly call Jesus *our Lord* without obeying Him?

Your Will be Done

Let your will be done is one of the most powerful prayers we can pray. It is both a prayer of surrender and a commitment to action. When we say these words, we are not asking God to sovereignly do His own will or to use other people instead of us, as if to say, "Let your will be done through other people as it is in heaven." On the contrary, when we pray this prayer, we are devoting our lives to personally doing His will no matter what it may cost us. Anything less is deception. For if we pray for God's will to be done, but do not truly want to do His will, then we are fooling ourselves that we even pray at all.

> **John 15:12-14, 17**
> "This is my commandment, that you love one another as I have loved you. Greater love has no one than this, that someone lay down his life for his friends. You are my friends if you do what I command you…These things I command you, so that you will love one another."

Everything that Jesus teaches us and every command He gives us has a single objective: to inspire us to love one another. It is the same for Paul, who writes that "the goal of our instruction is love from a pure heart."[3] It is the same for John who wrote his gospel so that we might have a life of love through faith in Jesus.[4] It is the same for every book that was ever written in union with Jesus. The goal of all true teaching is not merely to create a belief in a theology but to empower us to love. This is the will of God for all believers and it is the beginning of our obedience.

"Love one another as I have loved you."

In *First Love,* we saw how Jesus uses the Greek word *kathos* here to mean, "Love one another in exactly the same way that I have loved you." This is not simply a call to love *like* Jesus, as if we could generate our own Christlike love. No love that comes from our own good intentions will ever compare to His love. On the contrary, this is a call to love *with* Jesus. As channels of love, Jesus is calling us to live in union with Him and let Him pour out His love through us. So what is the love of Jesus like?

> **1 John 3:16-18**
> By this we know love, that he laid down his life for us, and we ought to lay down our lives for the brothers. But if anyone has the world's goods and sees his brother in need, yet closes his heart against him, how does God's love abide in him? Little children, let us not love in word or talk but in deed and in truth.

During His time on earth, Jesus always loved people by meeting their need. He fed the hungry, healed the sick, touched the untouchable, taught the uneducated, rebuked the hypocrites, gave honour to outcasts, shared wisdom with the unwise, and died to bring salvation to a world desperately in need of saving.

When Jesus gave His life for us, He showed us what His love is like: selfless, self-sacrificing and irresistible. The love of Christ holds nothing in reserve and acts with fierce resolve to achieve its goal. This is the love that Jesus wants to flows through us. It is so much more than just a feeling or disposition. It is a force of the nature of God within us that compels us to act selflessly to meet the needs of others.

Giving Without Fear

All throughout the world, it is common for people to give out of their excess to help those in need. Christians do not have a monopoly on love or giving, and both believers and unbelievers alike give because it feels good to give. Yet our call is not to love like the world but to love with Jesus. As long as we act like the world and limit our giving to the overflow of our wealth, we miss out on the joy of sacrificially loving with Jesus.

So why would we avoid His costly love? For many of us, there is a quiet fear at work. While we may want to start loving others by sacrificially giving to meet their needs, the voice of fear speaks: *How can you be sure if you give sacrificially that you will have enough for you and your family?*

Matthew 6:25-33

"Therefore I tell you, do not be anxious about your life, what you will eat or what you will drink, nor about your body, what you will put on. Is not life more than food, and the body more than clothing? Look at the birds of the air: they neither sow nor reap nor gather into barns, and yet your heavenly Father feeds them. Are you not of more value than they? And which of you by being anxious can add a single hour to his span of life? And why are you anxious about clothing? Consider the lilies of the field, how they grow: they neither toil nor spin, yet I tell you, even Solomon in all his glory was not arrayed like one of these. But if God so clothes the grass of the field, which today is alive and tomorrow is thrown into the oven, will he not much more clothe you, O you of little faith? Therefore do not be anxious, saying, 'What shall we eat?' or 'What shall we drink?' or 'What shall we wear?' For the Gentiles seek after all these things, and your heavenly Father knows that you need them all. But seek first the kingdom of God and his righteousness, and all these things will be added to you."

As the bride of Christ, we seek first the kingdom of God, devoting our lives to the wholehearted love of our king. As our husband, Jesus has promised to give us everything we need. This is not to say that we will never have any needs, but that God will always meet our needs. We never have to worry about what we will eat, where we will sleep, or what we will wear, ever again. **Jesus guarantees to take care of all our needs so we can be completely free to sacrificially love others.** Like the widow with two coins, if the Lord so leads us, we can give anything and everything we have without fear, for we have a Husband who loves us and who will always provide for our every need.

Depths of Love

In the shallows of love, we find words of affection and kindness; in the depths we find sacrificial giving to meet need. This is true for our relationships with other people, but what of our relationship with God?

We express our affection for Jesus in our prayers, our thoughts, and our songs of praise. But in terms of giving to meet needs, does Jesus have any needs in heaven? No. As the Word who is with God and who is God, Jesus is eternal, infinite, and entirely self-sufficient. So if Jesus has no need, then how can we ever know the depths of sacrificially loving Him?

In order to answer this question, we need to look at how our design of love works on a practical level.

One Plus Two Equals New

John 13:34-35

"A new commandment I give to you, that you love one another, just as I have loved you, you also are to love one another. By this all people will know that you are my disciples, if you have love for one another."

Here Jesus gives us the command to love one another and calls it the *new* command. But if loving God with all our heart is the greatest command, why did Jesus not command us to love God first? If we are created to be channels of the Father's love for Jesus, why make other people the focus of our love instead of Christ?

1 John 4:19-21

We love because he first loved us. If anyone says, "I love God," and hates his brother, he is a liar; for he who does not love his brother whom he has seen cannot love God whom he has not seen. And this commandment we have from him: whoever loves God must also love his brother.

2 Corinthians 13:5

Examine yourselves, to see whether you are in the faith. Test yourselves. Or do you not realise this about yourselves, that Jesus Christ is in you?—unless indeed you fail to meet the test!

God's design is that each one of us would live as a unique expression of His love for Jesus. And Jesus Christ lives within His people. This is worth repeating again and again: Jesus Christ lives within His people!

When Jesus gave us the new command, He was not making people the focus instead of God. On the contrary, Jesus was perfectly uniting the first and second commands of love, teaching us that because His Spirit dwells within His people, when we love one another, we love Him. This is why we are called to love one another so extravagantly and so fervently. When we love one another, we love God.

176

Sharing Needs, Sharing Love

Matthew 25:34-40

"Then the King will say to those on his right, 'Come, you who are blessed by my Father, inherit the kingdom prepared for you from the foundation of the world. For I was hungry and you gave me food, I was thirsty and you gave me drink, I was a stranger and you welcomed me, I was naked and you clothed me, I was sick and you visited me, I was in prison and you came to me.' Then the righteous will answer him, saying, 'Lord, when did we see you hungry and feed you, or thirsty and give you drink? And when did we see you a stranger and welcome you, or naked and clothe you? And when did we see you sick or in prison and visit you?' And the King will answer them, 'Truly, I say to you, as you did it to one of the least of these my brothers, you did it to me.'"

In *First Love,* we looked at this passage and saw how Jesus shares the needs of His people. Jesus experiences our pain, our sickness, and our bondage with us. And most of all, He shares our needs. Through His Spirit within us, God Almighty humbles Himself to be thirsty with us. The King of the Universe, who created both food and body, humbles Himself to share our hunger. Living with a need is a form of suffering, being uncomfortable at best and oftentimes painful. So why would Jesus want to share our discomfort?

By sharing our needs, Jesus also gets to experience the love we receive when someone meets our need. This is exactly how God intends His design of love to work. The Father created each one of us to share His love for Jesus *and* to be one with Christ so that we could genuinely love Jesus through one another.[5]

So while Jesus delights in our prayers and our songs, He does not want us to love Him only in words. On the contrary, **the primary way Jesus wants to receive our love is through His people.** And this requires so much more of us than just our words. It requires us to give our time, energy, money, and possessions to meet the needs of those around us. It calls us to be humble, patient, kind and selfless. It requires us to learn how to speak from the heart to the heart. Put simply, to love Christ through one another demands that we forge real relationships with one another, and this is almost guaranteed to be challenging, uncomfortable, unpredictable, messy and completely glorious.

As we seek to love Jesus more, we will naturally start to seek out need. A need could be financial, social, material, emotional, or practical. People may need money, food, friendship, encouragement, work, guidance, wisdom, help, clarity, or simply to have a little fun. A person might need help to discover and develop their unique giftings and calling. Another person might need some teaching to learn their eternal identity in Christ. Someone else might need to be reminded of the primacy of love.

If our hearts are filled with the Father's love for Jesus, we will naturally delight in meeting every need we can. The reason we keep love to ourselves is because we fail to perceive the presence of Christ within each other. If we only learned to see Jesus in His people, we would realise that every relationship we have with a believer is a potential channel of love between the Father and Son. So let us look for Jesus in His people, may the Fathers' love for Him burn within us, and may His love begin to flow!

Pray

Lord Jesus, I thank you for your call to love. Please help me to see your presence in your people and to minister to you through them. Help me to hold nothing back, but to let the love of the Father fully flow through me. Let your love come and your will be done. Let the riches of heaven be seen in the love of your saints.

Study Guide: page 237

28 | Believe and Love

The Father's love for Jesus only flows through us as we love one another. This was always God's original plan and as the parable of the sheep and goats shows us, it will be the basis for His ultimate judgment. This makes the call to love one another far more than extra credit for motivated Christians. It is an essential foundation for every believer's life.

> **1 John 3:23** (NASB)
> This is His commandment, that we believe in the name of His Son Jesus Christ and love one another, just as He commanded us.

The call to love is so vitally important that Scripture says there is only one command, with two parts:
1. that we believe in the name (nature) of His Son Jesus Christ, *and*
2. that we love one another.

The Bible makes it clear that we cannot obey God through faith alone—we must believe and act in love. And neither can we obey God through love alone—our acts of love must flow from faith, in relationship with Him. So what are we if we do not believe? We are unbelievers. And what are we if we do not love? Scripture says that life is only found in love, so if we do not love, we are more than disobedient—we are spiritually dead.[1]

> **Hebrews 10:24-25**
> And let us consider how to stir up one another to love and good works, not neglecting to meet together, as is the habit of some, but encouraging one another, and all the more as you see the Day drawing near.

None of us can obey the command to love one another in isolation. In order to love others, we need others. Therefore Scripture calls us to keep meeting together to spur each other on to love and good works. As the bride of Christ, we need to connect with other believers with our focus firmly set on loving Jesus through one another.

Love, Intimacy, Unity

Deuteronomy 30:19b-20a (adapted)
So choose life...by loving the LORD your God, by hearing His voice, and by becoming one with Him...

In *First Love,* we looked at the three pillars of life: love, intimacy and unity. These three pillars not only apply to our relationship with God, but they also define what it means to have life in our relationships with one another.

Between love and unity is the intimacy that comes from communicating with one another. Honest, heart-to-heart communication allows us to get to know one another and provides a platform for love in our relationships. And it starts with hearing. When we are slow to speak and quick to listen, we impart a sense of value to others, which immediately creates unity in the relationship. The more time we invest in simply talking honestly to each other, the more God's love can flow between us and make us one.

Real conversation connects us to one another and so it exists at the very heart of fellowship. This makes communication an essential part of our call of love. So imagine that instead of calling us to love one another, Jesus simply said, "This is my commandment: that you talk honestly to one another." How would this change the way we do our corporate meetings?

Matthew 18:19-20
Again I say to you, if two of you agree on earth about anything they ask, it will be done for them by my Father in heaven. For where two or three are gathered in my name, there am I among them."

The reality is that we do not have meaningful conversations in big groups. It goes against all our human psychology. In large groups, we may find a sense of community, but it comes at the cost of intimacy. As the number of people in a group increases, we naturally tend to guard our hearts more, hide our needs, and limit what we share of ourselves. But as our groups get smaller, we become less inhibited and our personalities start to shine. We become more honest and vulnerable with each other. And most importantly, as our groups get smaller and more intimate, they become more *loving*.

When Jesus called us to love one another, He did not expect us to gather hundreds or thousands of people at weekly services and call it love. He knows that we cannot truly love a crowd; we cannot have vulnerable conversations or meet one another's needs when we are gathered in large numbers. For this reason, Jesus establishes the twos and threes as the basic building block of His church. This is where love, conversation and unity are at their strongest. This is where the bride finds her home.

So is there a place for bigger meetings? Yes! But it is not at the expense of the small group meetings. Love must come first, which means that we need to focus primarily on our small group meetings and secondarily on our large meetings. Remember that our goal is to extravagantly love Jesus through His people. To be the most fruitful in love, we need to invest our greatest energy where love flows strongest: in the smallest groups. If we are faithful to meet in groups of two and three, we will then carry the love and unity that we forge in these relationships into our bigger group meetings, and it will be glorious beyond words.

So where do we start? The Early Church often met in homes because of their call to love one another. Meeting in a home allows for a sense of connecting as a family and provides a natural environment for conversation. However, in terms of His corporate design, God does not outline a specific structure, method or even place for our meetings. Why? Because God wants to build His church Himself. He wants us to listen to His voice without relying on a formula which could lead to us doing church without Him. He wants to be the head and have the freedom to lead us in the way that best lets

His love and goodness flow between us. Under His leadership we might meet in a home, an office, a café, a church building, a park, or even online. We may gather together for fellowship, teaching, study, sharing needs, worship, training, or working together. We may structure our groups differently as the Spirit leads us through different seasons with different people. Yet no matter how we do these groups, they will always have one foundation: Jesus Christ and His call of wholehearted love.

The Value in Love

1 Corinthians 13:1-3

If I speak in the tongues of men and of angels, but have not love, I am a noisy gong or a clanging cymbal. And if I have prophetic powers, and understand all mysteries and all knowledge, and if I have all faith, so as to remove mountains, but have not love, I am nothing. If I give away all I have, and if I deliver up my body to be burned, but have not love, I gain nothing.

We can prophesy all things, have all knowledge and understanding, we can give all we have; we can have faith to move mountains, we can cast out demons, and we can perform signs, wonders and miracles. But without love, everything we do counts for nothing. Without love, we are nothing.

Love alone gives value to every aspect of our lives, including our corporate meetings. If there is no flow of God's love between us, then our gatherings and religious services profit *nothing*. Our time here is short and we cannot afford to waste it on loveless traditions. We simply must meet together in a way that allows God's love to flow.

Small groups are the best way of creating true fellowship, however, we need to realise that like our bigger meetings, if our small groups lack love, then they will achieve nothing. They may be social and entertaining, even educational, but without love they are without value. It is therefore essential that our small groups have a clear and immovable focus on loving God through one another. If we continue to meet with a vision to spur each other on to love, it will not take long for new believers to mature from their infancy and to become one with Christ.

Love Attracts

John 13:35

"By this all people will know that you are my disciples, if you have love for one another."

God is love and so our unity with Him is revealed in love. For this reason, Jesus says that we will be recognised in the world by our love for one another. But do we really want this? If we do, we must accept that people do not typically experience love at big events or services. We only experience love through our relationships. So if we truly want to become known by our love for one another, then the primary expression of Christianity must move from the Sunday services to the small group meetings. The loving small group needs to become the face of evangelism. The loving small group needs to become the place of healing, discipleship, fellowship, training, equipping, miracles, and ministry. Such small groups must resist the temptation to become social groups, and instead become the place where the bride of Christ is prepared for her Bridegroom.[2]

When we build our fellowships on a foundation of love, we will find that the love of God is the most powerful and profoundly attractive thing in all creation. The irresistible nature of Christ's love was on full display when I was once at a home-fellowship meeting. A Muslim man was carried into the meeting by two people and set down in front of me. He was paralyzed down his left-hand side.

"God, what do I do with this?" I had never prayed for a paralyzed person before and had no idea how to pray.

"Pray for love," the Holy Spirit said in a clear thought. So I asked the man if he would like to feel how much Jesus loves him. He narrowed his dull eyes, looked at me suspiciously, and then gave the slightest nod. I prayed that Jesus would flood the man's heart with His love and fill every part of his being with love. I gave him some time to enjoy the love of Christ and then I spoke.

"Would you like to follow Jesus and have this love in your life all the time?"

With bright eyes, the man gave a big nod and said, "Yes please!" He was thirsty for real love. That night, he came to know Jesus as both his redeemer and his healer. After we prayed together, the man stood up and walked out, healed and redeemed by the love of Jesus. And all the glory went to God.

God has created us for a life of love. Because of this design, every person has an undeniable resonance with love. When non-believers feel the love of Christ or see His love in us, something in their hearts will witness to the fact that they too are designed for love.

This is how the bride of Christ will shine in the world. This is how she will share the gospel and bring the greatest delight to God. She will live a life of love, joy, and unity with her Bridegroom and her brethren, and that will attract people everywhere to His light. And it will be glorious.

Pray

Father, I thank you for this amazing design of love. Please share your vision for love with me. Help me to see what life looks like when we live according to your design of love. I thank you that your yoke is not just easy and light, but you made it to be delightful! Thank you that you want to fill me with joy as I love you through your people. Let's find that joy today.

29 | Bride Arise

As part of becoming the bride of Christ, we make our choice. We choose life. We choose to love God with our entire being and to accept all its far-reaching consequences. We make the first command the law of our life, and we make love our *Why*. Why do we meet together? Love. Why do we help others? Love. Why do we challenge each other? Love. Why do we refuse to gossip, judge, or condemn one another? Love. Why do we never give up on each other? Love. Our whole life is summed up by one small word that reveals the perfect nature of God and our glorious design: *Love*.

> **Jeremiah 13:11b**
> "...so I made the whole house of Israel and the whole house of Judah cling to me [*davaq: become one with*], declares the LORD, that they might be for me a people, a name, a praise, and a glory..."

> **John 17:20-23**
> "I do not ask for these only, but also for those who will believe in me through their word, that they may all be one, just as you, Father, are in me, and I in you, that they also may be in us, so that the world may believe that you have sent me. The glory that you have given me I have given to them, that they may be one even as we are one, I in them and you in me, that they may become perfectly one, so that the world may know that you sent me and loved them even as you loved me."

Just as He did for Israel, so God makes us one with Him so that we might be a name, a praise and a glory for Him. Jesus wants to lavish His bride with so much of His goodness and love that it radiates out of her to the world. He wants people of the world to see through us that Jesus is real, He has come, and He is altogether glorious. And it all starts with the unity of the bride and Bridegroom.

Isaiah 60:1-3

Arise, shine, for your light has come,

   and the glory of the LORD has risen upon you.

For behold, darkness shall cover the earth,

   and thick darkness the peoples;

   but the LORD will arise upon you,

   and his glory will be seen upon you.

And nations shall come to your light,

   and kings to the brightness of your rising.

Isaiah 62:2-4

The nations shall see your righteousness,

   and all the kings your glory,

   and you shall be called by a new name

   that the mouth of the LORD will give.

You shall be a crown of beauty in the hand of the LORD,

   and a royal diadem in the hand of your God.

You shall no more be termed Forsaken,

   and your land shall no more be termed Desolate,

   but you shall be called My Delight Is in Her,

   and your land Married;

   for the LORD delights in you,

   and your land shall be married.

A great darkness is covering the earth, but it is simply creating the conditions for the bride of Christ to arise and shine in all her glory. In the darkness of this selfish and fearful world, the bride will radiate His love and *masses* of people will be drawn to His light.

Love and Design

Earlier we learned how we only experience glory in our marriages when we submit to God's design of selfless love. We see this in Scripture when the glory of God falls upon the Tabernacle only after Moses arranges every detail according to God's perfect plan. This principle remains true: the only way to release glory is to align our lives with God's design.

As individuals, we know that God created us to become a bride for Christ, someone who could ravish His heart with a single look of her eyes. In every way, God has perfectly created us to be one with Him. In the same way, we need to know God's design for us corporately. Once we are confident of His corporate design, we need to fully commit to it.

Glory comes with unity, and there can be no unity without love. Many people make the mistake of trying to build unity without love. Some try to bring people together by creating common statements of faith, as if unity is based only on belief. Others try to unite different streams of Christianity by gathering people at a big service or event, as if unity is based on physical presence. Yet such efforts focus on the fruit rather than the root. Scripture is clear that love alone is the perfect bond of unity.[1] We do not become one with other believers by attending the same event, nor do we become one by making a membership pledge or signing a statement of belief. We only begin to become one with other believers when we start to genuinely love each other. Love is the only way to create unity and release glory. And love starts in small groups.

God's corporate design is for myriads of small groups to constantly meet with the goal of loving one another. These groups will undoubtedly come together in large meetings, but the large meetings will be secondary to the small. For the truth remains that the glory of God shines at its brightest where love is at its greatest: in small groups.

The Army Gathers

In the book *First Love,* I recounted the meeting I had with a woman who spent her days in prayer. She told me how God was bringing a great wave of His love across the islands, but this wave was only going to flow in small groups. She also told me of another vision, one that God had also already shown me.

"I see the sunrise over the beach. On the beach there is an army of believers, preparing to go to war."

The wave of God's love is going to flow across the nations, and many will find the grace to believe and become the bride of Christ. At the same time, there will be a great battle. This battle is not against people, but against the powers of darkness that keep people enslaved. This is a battle especially against the religious spirit, and as the army gains victory, the bondage of legalism will be broken. Many will be set free from their religious slavery to become both sons of God and brides of Christ.

The army of God is a group of believers who have learned how to overcome by the blood of the Lamb, the word of their testimony, and their selfless love. Each soldier in the army is willing to give their life for those they are fighting for and with.

All armies operate in strict obedience. No soldier is permitted to do their own will, but each one is bound to do the will of their commander. Obedience is the key to victory, and obedience starts with the greatest commands. Imagine a soldier who expected praise for staying in the barracks and cleaning his weapons when his primary orders were to engage the enemy. It is the same in the spirit. We cannot expect to please God by obeying the least commands if we neglect the greatest. *But Lord! I attended church every Sunday. I prayed faithfully. I gave money. I even cast out demons and healed the sick. Aren't you pleased?* None of these things counts for anything apart from love. The reality is that we only join the ranks of the army and know Jesus as our Lord when we start to obey His command to love.

Obedience and Authority

John 14:10

"Do you not believe that I am in the Father and the Father is in me? The words that I say to you I do not speak on my own authority, but the Father who dwells in me does his works."

Jesus lived in unity with the Father and so carried the Father's authority. Two keys to carrying the authority of God are submission and obedience. Like

Jesus, we need to submit to the Father, arranging everything in our lives according to His design. We then need to do His will. When we live in submission and obedience to the Father, the authority of God can be released through us.

The primary will of God is that we love Him through His people. If we are not actively loving one another then we are living in disobedience, which dramatically lessens our spiritual authority. However, when we start to come together in small groups and live out the first commands, we become "a royal diadem in the hand of God." Not only do we become channels of His love together, but we become channels of the awesome authority of God.

A friend called Silas shared a vision he had of a demonic power over Tahiti, which has influenced the whole region of Polynesia. It was a religious spirit that appeared as an octopus in dark clouds over the islands. Every time one of its tentacles touched the land, evil was released. A white dot appeared on the land, like a laser beam that extended from the heavens to the earth. Because of the intensity of the light, the tentacles of the octopus spirit were unable to pass through the light. Instead, the octopus had to twist its tentacles to go around the light. Then another white dot appeared, and another. Both the number and the intensity of these dots of lights grew. Eventually there was nowhere for the octopus to go. As it moved through the lights, its tentacles were burned away. Eventually the whole spirit was consumed, and the clouds cleared over the island. Silas looked at the dots of light and found that they were small groups of people who gathered together to love one another. These were groups that lived in submission and obedience to the Father. Their combined authority overcame the enemy and allowed the people of God to once again possess the gates of the land.

A Royal Diadem

Isaiah 62:3
You shall be a crown of beauty in the hand of the LORD,
and a royal diadem in the hand of your God.

Revelation 19:11-16

Then I saw heaven opened, and behold, a white horse! The one sitting on it is called Faithful and True, and in righteousness he judges and makes war. His eyes are like a flame of fire, and on his head are many diadems, and he has a name written that no one knows but himself. He is clothed in a robe dipped in blood, and the name by which he is called is The Word of God. And the armies of heaven, arrayed in fine linen, white and pure, were following him on white horses. From his mouth comes a sharp sword with which to strike down the nations, and he will rule them with a rod of iron. He will tread the winepress of the fury of the wrath of God the Almighty. On his robe and on his thigh he has a name written, King of kings and Lord of lords.

When we become the bride of Christ we come into a greater realm of spiritual beauty and authority in Christ. Like Esther, we exercise the highest authority not because of anything we have done, but because we live in an intimate union with the King of kings.

As His bride, we are one of many diadems upon the head of Christ. We are those who will war against the powers of darkness with Jesus and His armies. Through our unity with Him and our obedience to the commands of love, we will overcome. Our victory is inevitable. The religious spirit will be defeated, future brides will be set free, and it will be to His great glory. But we need to remember, we cannot carry this call or fight this fight alone. We must come together.

The One Another Project

Habakkuk 2:14

For the earth will be filled
with the knowledge of the glory of the LORD
as the waters cover the sea.

A woman called Magali shared a dream with me that God had given her. She saw herself on a beach, dressed as a bride. She then cast a net over the islands of the Pacific. In *First Love*, we looked at how God is weaving a massive net of Spirit-led small groups across the world. These groups are founded on the first commands and united by His love. These groups are His glory that will cover the earth like the waters cover the sea.

God is now casting his net through His bride. He is connecting people together who will love Him with all their heart and soul, and love one another. Because this net is made up of small groups, many will be hidden from public view. To enable people to connect to others in the net, we are starting the *One Another Project*. This is a website that lets people join with others in their area who have a heart to love.

The power of a net is its ability to absorb energy. For example, when an insect or bird flies into a silk web, the energy of the impact is spread throughout the entire net. The interconnected nature of the net makes it incredibly strong. Imagine being part of a massive net of people who are committed to meeting each other's needs. Imagine someone in your small group with a need that your group cannot meet alone. Imagine being able to share that need with other groups in the net, allowing the whole net to absorb the need. Our vision is for a net of people who love God with all their heart, love one another, *and have no need among them.*

If you would like to connect with a small group in your area, please visit www.oneanother.net

Pray

God, you are so awesome. May your glory cover the whole earth. May your bride arise and shine brightly with your love. May your people be drawn together in covenant love. May your net be cast, and may there be a great harvest of people that come to know you and love you. Please show me my part in all this. Please weave me into your net and connect me with people who I can love you through. I am yours.

30 | Freely Give

In many ways, the story of Sarah at the beginning of this book is a prophetic picture of this time we are living in. Sarah was enslaved for seven years, held captive by a man who himself was a captive of legalism. Though he called himself her husband, he was a cruel and vicious master. When faced with death, Sarah did not give in. Instead, she placed her life in God's hands. He saw her, freed her, and she ran away with Him. Sarah died to her life of slavery and was quickly reunited with her true husband, Daniel.

Like Sarah, so many believers are held captive by the chains of legalism, enslaved to a loveless husband. Even though they are well-intentioned, even zealous for God, so many are hopelessly trapped by the rules and traditions of legalism. But God is now waging war against legalism. He is coming for His bride, to break her chains, and to restore her to her true husband.

He is coming for you.

Freely Give

2 Corinthians 11:1-11

I wish you would bear with me in a little foolishness. Do bear with me! For I feel a divine jealousy for you, since I betrothed you to one husband, to present you as a pure virgin to Christ. But I am afraid that as the serpent deceived Eve by his cunning, your thoughts will be led astray from a sincere and pure devotion to Christ. For if someone comes and proclaims another Jesus than the one we proclaimed, or if you receive a different spirit from the one you received, or if you accept a different gospel from the one you accepted, you put up with it readily enough. Indeed, I consider that I am not in the least inferior to these super-apostles. Even if I am unskilled in speaking, I am not so in knowledge; indeed, in every way we have made this plain to you in all things.

Or did I commit a sin in humbling myself so that you might be exalted, because I preached God's gospel to you free of charge? I robbed other churches by accepting support from them in order to serve you. And when I was with you and was in need, I did not burden anyone, for the brothers who came from Macedonia supplied my need. So I refrained and will refrain from burdening you in any way. As the truth of Christ is in me, this boasting of mine will not be silenced in the regions of Achaia. And why? Because I do not love you? God knows I do!

Paul laboured like a eunuch for the King to betroth the people as a pure virgin to Christ. He refused to charge people for his ministry so that his gospel and ministry would not be limited. However, other teachers rose up within the Early Church who charged for their services but did not have the goal of preparing the bride for Jesus. Instead, they sought to make people dependent on their ministry. Instead of connecting the bride directly to her Bridegroom, they sought to mediate between the two. To make matters worse, the Corinthian believers started to value those ministers over Paul, in part because they charged for their ministry whereas Paul ministered for free. After all, you get what you pay for…right?

Paul affirmed that it is good for people who sow spiritually to reap materially. However, Paul did not want to limit the gospel in any way, especially through charging a fee. He knew that charging for his ministry would keep the message of covenant love out of the hands of those who are most likely to respond: the poor. Ironically, Paul had to defend himself for this position, even having to defend his love.

In terms of ministering to the bride, it is unthinkable that a eunuch would ever charge the bride for her preparation. He works for the king, and the king gives him what he needs. And God supplied all of Paul's needs in different ways, throughout his entire life.

It is with this heart that all the books in the *One with Christ* series are free. I have written this book for you. It is my gift of time, love and passion. My greatest hope is that as you have read it, you have found the grace to make a covenant with Jesus to love Him with all your heart and soul. It is my reward to help to increase the flow of love between the Father and the Son through you. My joy is to see the bride and her Bridegroom become one. So please, *please,* invest in your call. Make yourself ready and prepare as a bride. Let the Holy Spirit beautify and adorn you. Know that Jesus is not slow in keeping His promise. If you prepare, He will come, and you will be one with Christ. This is my profound joy in life.

I do not expect anything in return from you at all. I simply ask that if God has blessed you through this book, please share it with others. I would love to think that this book could help many people to become the bride of Christ in this life. To this end, I would like to invite you to share your testimony of coming into marriage to Jesus. The call of the bride can be difficult for some people to accept at first and reading your testimony may help someone to enter into their inheritance of love. If you would like to share your testimony, please email bride@onewithchrist.org

Seeking Fruit

Philippians 4:17
Not that I seek the gift, but I seek the fruit that increases to your credit.

Our focus is on seeking fruit that remains. There is no charge for our ministry, and we do not want you to feel any sense of obligation to give. However, if you feel led to support us as we prepare the bride for Jesus, then please connect with us. We have three key projects that dovetail together to prepare the bride in different ways.

Freeslaves.org

Freeslaves.org is a project that primarily focuses on redeeming Christian families from bonded-labour slavery. We pay their debts and arrange work for the families. If they are willing, we then connect the families with other believers for discipleship, with the focus of preparing the bride for covenant love and unity with Jesus. We also run a number of schools for enslaved children and provide aid to those in need.

Days before I first visited Pakistan, I came from sharing the call of the bride with a small group of western believers, living in Nepal. At the end of the Bible study, the people thanked me for my time: *Thanks for sharing, that was really interesting.* Days later I was in Pakistan, speaking to a group of around 200 believers. I again called the bride to prepare. After I had shared, someone else spoke. *People, we have to respond! God is calling us to become His bride. If you would like to make a covenant with God to love Him with all your heart and soul, come and we will pray with you.* Almost 150 out of 200 people came forward. They were hungry for love.

I realised that in the West we have been trained to receive teaching on an intellectual level. We expect to learn about God rather than encounter Him. We are taught to receive from God but not to give to Him. As a result, we think that our wealth, comfort and entertainment are all blessings from God.[1] Yet these "blessings" can too easily combine to make us complacent with God. We hear the call of the bride and we take it casually. *Thanks, that was interesting.* It is simply so hard for the rich to enter the kingdom of God and become a bride of selfless love.

Most believers in Pakistan are not bound by complacency. Pakistan is home to some of the poorest believers on the planet and God has chosen these poor to be rich in faith.[2] These are the ones that are quick to respond to the call of the bride. The harvest is ready. The bride is waiting. If you would like to help us to lift the bride out of her slavery and connect her to her Bridegroom, please consider supporting freeslaves.org

Acacia Media (www.acacia.media)

This project includes all our writing, media, and translation work from our websites, including onewithchrist.org. Our vision is to establish Acacia Media with a specific focus on freely publishing media that honours the place of the first and second commands of love and prepares the bride for Jesus.

One Another Project (www.oneanother.net)

Jesus calls us to love one another. However, we cannot love a crowd. Instead, we can only love in small groups, starting with twos and threes. As mentioned in the last chapter, this website provides a way for people to connect to small groups in their area that are founded on love. It also provides resources for small group study. If you have started a group or you would like to connect with a group in your area, please feel free to visit www.oneanother.net

If you would like to support any of these projects, please visit

acaciaprojects.org/donate

Final Words

May the God of peace, love and grace bless you beyond all reason. May the Spirit of God adorn you and prepare you as the bride for your Bridegroom. May you ascend the stairs and find your Bridegroom in the secret place. May your heart be made as pure as light, and may the Spirit make you beautiful beyond words. May Christ Himself be captivated by your love and ravished with just one look from your eyes. May He delight in you as His bride and rejoice over you with singing. May you become the living glory of your Husband. May the earth tremble at the sight of your beauty and the greatness of God's goodness in your life. May you be a pure and ever-expanding channel of the Father's love for Jesus. May you delight in loving Jesus through His people. May you become more one with Christ as you live in covenant with Him. And may we all celebrate your marriage to the Lamb together in eternity.

Small Groups

As the Bride of Christ, our overarching goal is to love Jesus more. We know that Christ's desire is that we would love Him through His people, and we want to be quick to respond to that desire. We start by forming heart-to-heart connections with other believers where we can encourage one another in love and meet each other's needs. Love flows strongest in the smallest numbers and so the best place to begin is in a small group.

Teams

The word *Team* is a term we use to describe groups of between two and four people who are devoted to living in God's design of love. The goal of meeting in these groups is to:
- actively spur each other on to love, which involves:
    - being accountable to the commands of love
    - encouraging each other to greater depths of intimacy and unity with Jesus
    - praying for healing and empowerment through the Spirit and investing in each other's lives
- live in the light with one another, which involves:
    - confessing any sin
    - sharing victories over temptation
    - honestly expressing your heart with one another

The following questions are designed to help you and the people in your team grow in their love, intimacy, and unity with Jesus.[1] You do not need to ask all these questions every time you meet, but instead be free to follow the leading of the Holy Spirit and add your own questions. Everything that is shared in the group should remain in strict confidence.

Have you sinned in the last week?

It is important when confessing sin to each other to show grace to one another, releasing the assurance of forgiveness and the cleansing power of the blood of Jesus to wash away all sin. In most cases, the confession of sin will bring a real sense of freedom and joy.

Have you faced any temptations over the last week? How did you overcome those temptations?

Temptations will often come, and it is important to create an expectation of overcoming in the face of temptation.

Did you do anything in the last week that you were unsure of whether it was righteous or sinful?

This question explores the grey areas in life where the enemy may try to seduce or distract us, or where the Lord may be working.

Is there anything in your life you would rather keep hidden?

The more transparent we become with each other, the more we will experience the joy of being truly known and loved by one another. There is amazing freedom to be found in being transparent with one another, however at first, people may find it difficult to share honestly with others. Living in the light feels vulnerable and requires great humility, so we need to always respond with real grace and love and keep encouraging each other in the pursuit of love.

How did you express the love of God over the last week?

This question helps us to focus on sharing the love of God with others.

Did you miss any opportunities to love over the last week?

This question helps us to be accountable for the opportunities that the Lord gives us to express His love for people.

Did you share God's joy over the last week?

This question reminds us of how Jesus longs to share His great joy with us.

Did you increase your capacity for love over the last week?

This question focuses on taking risks when loving others. It also helps us to view relational challenges (such as betrayal or offense) as opportunities to increase our capacity for love.

Have you been hearing the voice of God over the last week? What has He been saying? Have you obeyed His voice?

This question creates space to share about our own intimacy with Jesus.

If Jesus were here and asked, "What do you want me to do for you?" what would you say?

This question challenges us to share our deepest desires and helps us to truly get to know each other.

Have you been able to think "We" over the last week?

This reminds people to account for the unity they share with Jesus in the way they think. It is a simple and effective way to involve Jesus in everyday life.

Have you met the needs of others over the last week?

This question focuses us on the practical expressions of love.

Do you have any needs?

This gives us the chance to truly love each other by meeting each other's needs.

In what way can we encourage you or help you in your spiritual growth?

This question allows the team to explore the different ways that we can help one another to pursue maturity in Christ.

Fellowship Groups

These groups are like families of faith and can be any size up to 20 people, though 12 is close to ideal. The focus of these groups is on loving one another, fellowship, teaching, worship, encouragement, ministry, and on sharing the gospel. Within the conversations that take place between people in such meetings, we suggest asking questions like the following:

How have you loved others over the last week? Have you found joy in loving others?
These questions invite us to share a testimony of the love of God in our lives.

Have you been delighting in God, in His word, in prayer, and in worship?
This question explores our relationship with God and helps us to focus on finding our joy and delight in Christ.

How has the Lord been speaking to you lately? What has He been saying?
This question creates an expectancy regarding hearing the voice of God.

How are you pursuing your design of love (loving God with all your being, and loving Him through others)?
This question keeps the greatest command in focus.

Have you faced any distractions in the pursuit of love and holiness? How did you overcome those distractions?
This question acknowledges that the enemy will be constantly trying to hinder us from living in our design of love. It also creates the expectation that we will overcome those distractions with the help of God.

Have you faced discouragement or the temptation to isolate this week?
These are two common strategies of the enemy to lead us away from love.

What qualities of Christ's character do you want to grow in?

This question helps us to remember that Jesus always wants to share more of Himself with us.

What do you need?

This is another way of asking, "how can I love you?"

Special Focus Groups

These groups are formed for a specific purpose for a season. They are usually based around a gifting or ministry and can be used to develop maturity in a specific area of spiritual life. For example, the Lord may lead someone in a team or fellowship group to begin a worship group. Those who feel led to participate can then join in. These special focus groups are a key way to help people to grow in their calling. They give people the opportunity to mature by practising using their gifts and expressing their unique love for Jesus.

These groups can be many and varied. The focus of such groups may include:
- helping others to learn how to move in their spiritual gifts
- sharing the gospel with new or non-believers
- praise and worship
- prayer ministry
- missions
- teaching and theology groups
- community ministry groups
- project groups

We would encourage you both to invest deeply in a weekly team meeting and a fellowship group meeting in your area. More resources for small groups can be found online at oneanother.net.

Get the Next Book!

If you have been blessed by *Bride Arise,* then please know that there is more blessing waiting to be discovered in the next book: *And He Will.*

And He Will

This book focuses on our progression into covenant love. In it we learn how to access God's promise to circumcise our heart and bring us into the reality of wholehearted love and unity with Him. Some have said this is the best book of the series, so be sure to read it and experience a deeper realm of covenant love, purity and unity with Jesus.

And He Will is available for free at **onewithchrist.org**

www.onewithchrist.org

Study Guide

This book has been written to prepare the reader as a bride for Jesus. A key part of this preparation is making time to connect with the Lord and commune with Him. This section contains questions and meditations to help you to do this. These can be used for personal or group study, and you are of course free to write your own questions or meditate on different Scriptures for each chapter.

Reflect

This section contains searching questions that are designed to explore the heart. The more thought you give to these questions, the more helpful they will be in inspiring you to grow spiritually. So take your time as you reflect on these questions and ask the Holy Spirit to prepare your heart for Jesus as you do them. It is His role to lead us into reality, so we can trust Him to give us the revelation, insight and love we need to become a bride of surpassing beauty for Jesus.

Write

For those readers who have not read *First Love*, in these sections we ask God a question. We then we ask the Holy Spirit to sanctify our minds and share the thoughts of God with us in response, writing down the thoughts that come to mind. If this seems strange to you, take some time to look at the Biblical background of sharing the thoughts of God in *First Love*.

You only have one mind to share with Jesus so these thoughts will sound like your own, but they will express the heart of God in a unique way. After you have finished, you can test what you have written by comparing it to the word of God, the witness of the Spirit, the sense of life, and the standard of the first commands of love. See *First Love* to learn more about hearing and testing the thoughts of God.

Imagine

Scripture calls us to meditate on the word of God and impress the truth on our hearts. In these sections, we focus on a portion of Scripture and allow the Holy Spirit to inspire our imagination and help us to picture the truth of Scripture as a reality in our lives. This is not like the fantasy of daydreaming, and it is not like New-Age or Eastern meditation where people empty their minds. This is Biblical meditation, where we fill our minds with the truth and reality of God. We look more at the importance of using our imagination in Chapter 13 and in the book *First Love*.

1. Design of Love

Please read the Study Guide introduction before beginning.

Reflect

Do I really believe that I am designed for love?

What would it feel like to share Jesus' love for the Father?

What does it mean for me to live in union with Jesus?

Am I ready to devote my whole life to loving God with my entire being?

Write

Jesus, will you share your love for the Father with me? Can we love Him in unity with all our heart and soul?

Imagine

Matthew 22:37-40 (BSB)

Jesus declared, "'Love the Lord your God with all your heart and with all your soul and with all your mind.' This is the first and greatest commandment. And the second is like it: 'Love your neighbour as yourself.' All the Law and the Prophets depend on these two commandments.'"

Take some time to memorise this passage, then start to meditate on it. Imagine Jesus speaking these words to you. Invite the Holy Spirit to make it real for you. Imagine the Spirit of Jesus filling every part of your being with one goal: to love the Father. Imagine feeling His love for the Father fill your heart, soul, mind and body. Imagine being one with Him.

2. Eternal Reality of Love

Reflect

Do I believe in the love that Jesus and the Father have for me?

Do I want to have the Father's love for Jesus in my life?

Do I have the faith for this kind of love?

How can I receive the Father's love for Jesus?

Write

Father, will you share your love for Jesus with me in this life?

Imagine

John 17:26 (BSB)
"And I have made Your name known to them and will continue to make it known, so that the love You have for Me may be in them, and I in them."

Ask the Spirit to inspire your imagination and bring revelation to your heart. Memorise this verse. Speak it out loud and listen to the sound of the words. Now take ten minutes to meditate only on this verse. Go through it slowly. Imagine Jesus praying these words. Imagine the Father's response. Imagine Jesus holding your hand right now and praying these words to the Father over you, using your name.

"Father, I have made known your name to _____, and I will continue to make it known, so that your love for me may live in _____, and I in him/her."

Now imagine the Father hearing Jesus' prayer and releasing His love for Jesus into you. Imagine what it feels like to have the consuming intensity of the Father's love flowing through your heart and soul. Imagine being alive in love.

3. Unique in Love

Reflect

What does it mean for me to be created for Jesus?

Have I been fitting God into my life, or my life into God's design?

Do I think of myself as an expression of the Father's love?

Does God look at me and think that I am very good?

Write

Father, did You really create me as an expression of Your love for Jesus? Can I really become a channel of your love for Him?

Imagine

Colossians 1:15-17

He [Jesus] is the image of the invisible God, the firstborn of all creation. For by him all things were created, in heaven and on earth, visible and invisible, whether thrones or dominions or rulers or authorities—all things were created through him and for him. And he is before all things, and in him all things hold together.

Imagine the Father creating the universe and everything in it as a gift of love for Jesus. Imagine Him creating you as one of His most precious gifts for Jesus. Imagine the Father preparing you and presenting you to Jesus as a gift of His awesome love.

4. Value in Love

Reflect

If true value is found in love, am I rich or poor right now?

Can I increase my value to God?

Is the life of a non-believer valuable to God?

Is there anyone I need to forgive?

Write

Father, I want to enter into my full value today, as much as my faith will allow. How can I love Jesus with your love today?

Imagine

Matthew 10:31

"Fear not, therefore; you are of more value than many sparrows."

Imagine Jesus speaking these words to you with a smile. Then imagine Him going to the cross in your place. *You are worth more than many sparrows. You are worth my life.*

Now imagine the Spirit of Jesus clearing all your debts and restoring your true value. Imagine Him pouring out the Father's love for Jesus into you. Imagine what it feels like to have that love flow through you. Imagine Jesus receiving that love.

Act

If you need to forgive someone, write them a letter or email. Ask God to give you the words to write. Do it as an act of obedience to God. If there is grace, send it.

5. Into our Inheritance

Reflect

What is a blessing that God has led me to experience recently?

What blessings are still on my gift-shelf, waiting to be unwrapped?

What is a truth or promise that I would like to experience as a reality?

How can I receive revelation from God?[1]

Write

Father, what blessing would you like to give me today?

Imagine

Isaiah 1:19 (BSB)
If you are willing and obedient, you will eat the best of the land.

Imagine your life as the Promised Land, a place of spiritual abundance and fruitfulness. Imagine a life of selfless love and joy. Imagine taking a journey into the life that God has prepared for you. Imagine willingly obeying every leading of the Holy Spirit as He leads you to experience the best of the land.

6. You Alone

Reflect

In what way do I prefer to relate to God?

Do I know God as my Father?

What is the difference between knowing Jesus as my friend and knowing Him as my bridegroom?

What does the marriage relationship with Jesus require of me?

Write

God, what relationship are you wanting to take me deeper into with you in this season? And what is our next step?

Imagine

> Psalm 27:4-5
>
> One thing have I asked of the LORD,
>   that will I seek after:
> that I may dwell in the house of the LORD
>   all the days of my life,
> to gaze upon the beauty of the LORD
>   and to inquire in his temple.

Like David, we can have the joy of beholding the beauty of God. One way of doing this is to take an aspect of His nature, such as His goodness or love or faithfulness or joy, and then meditate on it by going to the very limits of our imagination. In their extreme, every quality of God is irresistibly attractive and beautiful. As we fully engage our imagination, we can feel safe knowing that God is better than we could ever imagine. He is more loving than we could ever dream. So choose an aspect of God's nature, and take some time to push your imagination to its very limits.

7. A Time for Love

Reflect

Where am I in the process of growth from infancy to maturity?

Is it really possible to know Jesus as my bridegroom in this life?

Does Jesus want to adorn and beautify me? What would that look like?

What does it mean to succeed to royalty through love?

Do I want to become known for my love?

Write

Jesus, are you calling me to become your bride?

Imagine

Jeremiah 31:3 (BSB)

The LORD appeared to him from afar: "I have loved you with an everlasting love; therefore I have drawn you with loving devotion."

Imagine Jesus saying these words to you: *"I have loved you with an everlasting love; I have drawn you with loving devotion."* Write them on your heart. Imagine living with complete confidence in the eternal love that Jesus has for you. Imagine knowing that nothing can ever separate you from His love— that you were created through His love, you are sustained by His love, and you will live for all eternity in His love.

8. Covenant of Love

Reflect

Am I ready to make a covenant with Jesus?

Is there anything in my heart that resists His love?

Is it possible for God to cut everything out my heart that resists His love?

What would it be like to live in union with Jesus?

Write

Father, have you betrothed me to Jesus?

Imagine

Song of Solomon 7:10
"I am my beloved's, and his desire is for me."

Let these words soak into your heart. Imagine Jesus, burning with desire for you. Imagine Him inviting you to make a covenant with Him. Imagine Jesus speaking the words to you, *"I betroth you to me forever. I betroth you to me in righteousness and in justice, in steadfast love and in mercy. I betroth you to me in faithfulness. You shall know Me."*

Act

If you want to experience the marriage covenant with God, then take some time now and get engaged! Promise to love and obey Him with all your heart, soul, mind and strength. Ask for His grace so that you might be faithful to keep your covenant. Then prepare for the thrill of falling in love! Declare that you will be married to God, you will be one with Christ, for this is His desire and He will do it!

9. One with Christ

Reflect

What are the consequences of saying *"yes"* to the first command?

What does it mean to share one spirit with Jesus?

How can this become real for me?

What would it be like to think and feel in unity with Jesus?

Write

Jesus, today I would specifically like to exchange _____ with you. Would you please take this out of my life? What would you like to give me in exchange?

Imagine

2 Peter 1:4

...He has granted to us his precious and very great promises, so that through them you may become partakers of the divine nature, having escaped from the corruption that is in the world because of sinful desire...

Imagine partaking of the divine nature. Imagine the very nature of Christ overtaking you with love. Imagine drinking His life. Imagine His blood flowing through you, energising your inner-being and washing all the corruption of the world away from you. Imagine feeling alive.

Act

Take some bread and wine and commune with Jesus today. Make it a prophetic statement of your devotion to unity and wholehearted love.

10. Preparing for Love

Reflect

Does my prayer-life express a desire to grow in love?

How do I feel when I worship God? Why?

Am I harbouring any sin or unforgiveness in my heart?

Is there a pattern of sin in my life that needs to be dealt with at the root?

Write

Holy Spirit, is there a lie I am believing or a sin that I am hiding that you want to expose and deal with today?

Is there a particular quality of Christ that you'd like me to put on today?

Imagine

Colossians 3:12-14 (BSB)

Therefore, as the elect of God, holy and beloved, clothe yourselves with compassion, kindness, humility, gentleness, and patience. Bear with each other and forgive any complaint you may have against one another. Forgive as the Lord forgave you. And over all these virtues put on love, which is the bond of perfect unity.

Imagine God opening a wardrobe of His finest clothes, with each garment representing a different quality of His nature. Imagine Him offering you a garment of compassion. Imagine putting it on and feeling the compassion of Christ fill your heart. Imagine clothing yourself with kindness and humility and feeling your pride melt away. Which qualities of Christ are most attractive to you? Which ones make you the most beautiful? What will you wear today?

11. The Ten Virgins

Reflect

How can I get more oil in my life?

Am I spending time in the Scriptures?

Is it easy or hard for me to spend time waiting on God?

Write

Father, I long to be like a wise virgin. What is one piece of wisdom that you would like to share with me today?

Imagine

Matthew 25:10-12

"And while they were going to buy, the bridegroom came, and those who were ready went in with him to the marriage feast, and the door was shut. Afterward the other virgins came also, saying, 'Lord, lord, open to us.' But he answered, 'Truly, I say to you, I do not know you.'"

Being foolish is different than being wicked. The wicked suffer judgment, but the foolish suffer loss. Imagine living a casual life with God and letting the distractions of the world consume your time and focus. Then imagine encountering Jesus and catching a glimpse of the glory of the bride and bridegroom. Imagine seeing the eyes of Jesus, burning with fire as He looks into His bride's eyes. Then imagine Jesus turning to you with tear-filled eyes. Imagine listening to Him saying through tears, "I'm sorry. You made your choice. This is not for you. I love you, but I do not know you." Imagine Jesus closing the door on you.

Now imagine that there is still time to become wise and prepare as a bride. How are you going to live? What will you choose?

12. Love and Humility

Reflect

Can I be both loving and proud at the same time?

Can I see any pride in my life?

Can other people see any pride in me?

Would God really oppose me because of pride?

Write

Father, how can I humble myself before you and before others today?

Imagine

Psalm 33:6
By the word of the LORD the heavens were made,
and by the breath of his mouth all their host.

Imagine watching God create the universe and breathe galaxies into being. Imagine hearing the roar of creation as God spreads out the heavens. Imagine feeling the heat as new stars are created. Imagine the colour and brightness of the universe in all its glory.

Now imagine a God who is so infinitely more glorious, a God who exists in a state so unimaginably awesome; imagine this God having to humble Himself to look at the splendour of the universe He created.

Now imagine Jesus, through whom and for whom all creation came into being, humbling Himself to wash your feet. Imagine feeling the water and hearing the sound as He gently cleanses you. Imagine watching the dust wash away and feeling His hands upon you. Imagine Him looking up into your eyes and smiling.

13. Undistracted Devotion

Reflect

How much do I love Jesus?

How do I usually worship Jesus? Is my worship costly?

How can I worship Jesus in a deeper, more costly way?

Write

Jesus, what does it mean for me to wash your feet?

Imagine

Luke 7:36-39 (NKJV)

Then one of the Pharisees asked Him⌒ to eat with him. And He went to the Pharisee's house, and sat down to eat. And behold, a woman in the city who was a sinner, when she knew that Jesus sat at the table in the Pharisee's house, brought an alabaster flask of fragrant oil, and stood at His feet behind Him weeping; and she began to wash~ His feet with her tears, and wiped them⌒ with the hair of her head; and she kissed⌒ His feet and anointed⌒ them with the fragrant oil. Now when the Pharisee who had invited Him saw this, he spoke to himself, saying, "This Man, if He were a prophet, would know who and what manner of woman this is who is touching Him, for she is a sinner."

Ask the Holy Spirit to sanctify your imagination and then take a few minutes to meditate on this passage. Let the Holy Spirit bring life to your senses and emotions as you imagine what it would be like to be in the room, watching the scene unfold. Then imagine what it would be like to be in the place of the woman. Imagine giving Jesus your most precious possession. Imagine pushing through your own brokenness and pain, and simply washing Jesus' feet.

14. Dying to the Law

Reflect

Have I been trying to earn God's blessing or love?

Do I believe that God is always good and that He likes me?

Do I want to be completely free from striving?

How can I die to the Law?

Write

Father, am I believing any lies of legalism? Are there any agreements with legalism that I need to break?

Imagine

Galatians 2:19-20

For through the law I died to the law, so that I might live to God. I have been crucified with Christ. It is no longer I who live, but Christ who lives in me. And the life I now live in the flesh I live by faith in the Son of God, who loved me and gave himself for me.

Read over this passage slowly. Take a minute to memorise it. Imagine dying to the law and being set free to live completely for God. Imagine being crucified with Christ and feeling all selfishness die within you. Imagine living in union with Jesus.

Extra Reading

If God is speaking to you regarding legalism, consider taking some time to revisit chapters 17-20 of *First Love*.

15. Leaving the Vineyard

Reflect

Am I desperate for Jesus?

What does it mean for me to leave the vineyard?

What is my next step in ascending to find Jesus in the secret place?

What are the main distractions that challenge my ascent to love?

Write

Holy Spirit, what is my next step as I ascend with You?

Imagine

Song of Songs 2:10-13
Shulamite
"My beloved responded and said to me:
'Arise, my darling, my beautiful one, and come away.
　For behold, the winter is past, the rain is over and gone.
The flowers have already appeared in the land;
　The time has arrived for pruning the vines,
　And the voice of the turtledove has been heard in our land.
The fig tree has ripened its figs,
　And the vines in blossom have given forth their fragrance.
Arise, my darling, my beautiful one, and come away!
O my dove, in the clefts of the rock,
　In the secret place of the steep pathway,
　Let me see your form, let me hear your voice;
　For your voice is sweet, and your form is lovely.'"

Imagine Jesus saying these words to you. Imagine Him calling you to arise and come with Him. Imagine hearing His voice, calling you to ascend the steep pathway. Imagine answering His call.

219

16. Sarah Must Die

Reflect

What does it mean to be spiritually beautiful?

How can I become more extravagant in my love and giving?

Have I died to the Law?

Do I want to be completely free from legalism?

Write

Holy Spirit, how can I become more like Rebekah—more generous, more humble, more courageous, and more beautiful?

Imagine

Colossians 2:13-14

And you, who were dead in your trespasses and the uncircumcision of your flesh, God made alive together with him, having forgiven us all our trespasses, by cancelling the record of debt that stood against us with its legal demands. This he set aside, nailing it to the cross.

Imagine Jesus taking your record of debt—all the things that you should be and should do—and nailing it to the cross. Imagine Him saying to you, *"The power of legalism is forever cancelled in your life. I free you from ever feeling like you need to earn my affection. I free you from all shame, all guilt, and all condemnation. Know that I love you with an everlasting love. You are my bride and my beloved now and forever."*

Imagine Jesus filling your heart with His love.

17. Let Him

Reflect

Is there anyone at all in my life who I need to forgive?

Am I holding on to any sense of injustice?

Are there any resistances to love in my life?

Have I made any agreements that have capped the wells of love?

How easy is it for me to believe that God loves me with an everlasting love?

Write

Father, what is a resistance to love that you would like to overcome in me today?

Imagine

2 Corinthians 10:4-5

For the weapons of our warfare are not of the flesh but have divine power to destroy strongholds. We destroy arguments and every lofty opinion raised against the knowledge of God, and take every thought captive to obey Christ.

Imagine the Spirit of God destroying all the strongholds, opinions, and arguments you have that stand against the intimate knowledge of God. Imagine Him giving you the grace to forgive and to let go of your past and your pain. Imagine Him restoring your capacity to receive love and to love freely.

18. With One Look

Reflect

Do I really believe that I am perfectly designed for love?

Do I believe that the Father loves me just as much as He loves Jesus?

What would it feel like for the Father's love for Jesus to flow through me?

How hungry am I for this?

Write

Jesus, how does the love of the bride feel for you?

Imagine

Song of Solomon 4:9 (NKJV)
"You have ravished my heart,
My sister, my spouse;
You have ravished my heart
With one look of your eyes,
With one link of your necklace."

Take some time to memorise this verse. Imagine looking into the eyes of Jesus. Imagine the Father's love for Jesus flowing through you. Imagine Jesus feeling completely captivated and undone by the love you share with Him.

19. Seeking out the Bride

Reflect

What would it look like for me to call the bride?

How would it feel to see someone fall in love with Jesus?

Am I ready to fight for the bride of Christ?

Write

Father, is there anyone that needs to hear this message about becoming your bride? If so, how can I share this message with them?

Imagine

Revelation 22:17

The Spirit and the Bride say, "Come." And let the one who hears say, "Come." And let the one who is thirsty come; let the one who desires take the water of life without price.

Imagine joining with the Holy Spirit to call the people to come! Imagine seeing thirsty people come to Jesus and drink the water of life. Imagine what it would feel like to see people fall in love with Him.

20. Eunuchs for the Kingdom

Reflect

Do I feed on people's praise or respect?

Am I willing to embrace obscurity so that I can prepare the bride for Jesus?

Am I willing to pour myself out for the bride of Christ?

Are there any shiny wrappers that are distracting me at the moment?

Write

Father, how can I grow in love and faithfulness?

Imagine

Proverbs 3:3
Let not steadfast [covenant] love and faithfulness forsake you;
    bind them around your neck;
    write them on the tablet of your heart.

Proverbs 19:22
What is desired in a man is steadfast [covenant] love,
    and a poor man is better than a liar.

Imagine writing the covenant of love and faithfulness on your heart. Imagine it encompassing your will. Imagine that the only thing that God desires from you is covenant love. Imagine Him saying to you, *"The only thing I will ever require of you is simply that you love me with all your heart and soul. And if you will say 'Yes' to me, I will make it a reality."*

21. Bride or Babe?

Reflect

What does it mean for Jesus to be my bridegroom of blood?

How is the circumcision of the heart connected to the covenant of the bride?

Do I have the courage of Ruth to pursue marriage to Jesus?

Write

Lord, have you given me the keys to the kingdom of heaven? If so, how can I use them?

Imagine

Luke 11:52

"Woe to you lawyers! For you have taken away the key of knowledge. You did not enter yourselves, and you hindered those who were entering."

Matthew 16:19

"I will give you the keys of the kingdom of heaven, and whatever you bind on earth shall be bound in heaven, and whatever you loose on earth shall be loosed in heaven."

Imagine holding the keys to the kingdom of heaven in your hand. Knowledge is the key to the kingdom. Imagine using the knowledge that God has given you to bind legalism and expose false doctrine. Imagine sharing the truth with someone and seeing them set free to become the bride of Christ.

22. Bride to Be?

Reflect

What if we are wrong? What are the consequences of wrongly believing that we can love Jesus with all our heart and become His bride in this life?

What if we are right? What are the consequences of *not* believing that we can love Jesus with all our heart and become His bride in this life?

Write

Father, I want to be dressed in the best wedding clothes possible. What would you like to clothe me in today?

Imagine

Isaiah 4:3-4

And he who is left in Zion and remains in Jerusalem will be called holy, everyone who has been recorded for life in Jerusalem, when the LORD shall have washed away the filth of the daughters of Zion and cleansed the bloodstains of Jerusalem from its midst by a spirit of judgment and by a spirit of burning.

God's judgment is His love. It separates good and evil within us and burns away all that is not pleasing in His sight. Imagine God coming to you as your judge. Imagine Him passing judgment on everything that has been holding you back from love. Imagine every unclean thing within your heart and soul burn away in the consuming fire of His love.

23. Redeeming the Bride

Reflect

Do I fear legalism or license? Should I?

Am I listening to teaching that honours the first command?

If a teaching is true, could it still be a distraction?

Am I confident that God will always restore me into His love if I fall?

Write

Father, how can I press on to know you today?

Imagine

Hosea 6:1-3
"Come, let us return to the LORD;
  for he has torn us, that he may heal us;
  he has struck us down, and he will bind us up.
 After two days he will revive us;
  on the third day he will raise us up,
  that we may live before him.
 Let us know; let us press on to know the LORD;
  his going out is sure as the dawn;
  he will come to us as the showers,
  as the spring rains that water the earth."

Let us press on to know the Lord. Imagine returning to the Lord and imagine Him reviving your heart. Imagine him raising you up to walk in His love. Imagine having the confidence that no matter what happens, God will always be there to revive you. Imagine pressing on to know the Lord.

24. Learning to Live in Love

Reflect

How can I practically express the love of God?

How can I build my intimacy with Jesus?

How can I learn to think *We?*

How will thinking *We* change the way I live?

Write

Lord, what is one area of my life that you are calling me to think "We"?

Imagine

Galatians 2:20

I have been crucified with Christ. It is no longer I who live, but Christ who lives in me. And the life I now live in the flesh I live by faith in the Son of God, who loved me and gave himself for me.

Take some time to memorise this verse. Imagine truly believing that it is "no longer I." Imagine being so aware of the presence of Christ within you that you naturally think *We.* How does that look? How does it feel?

25. Bride and Glory

Imagine

Jeremiah 33:9

"And this city shall be to me a name of joy, a praise and a glory before all the nations of the earth who shall hear of all the good that I do for them. They shall fear and tremble because of all the good and all the prosperity I provide for it."

Imagine the Father speaking these words over you: *Your name shall be a name of joy; a praise and a glory in the world, for people will hear of all the extravagant goodness that I am doing for you. They shall be in awe over the prosperity I bring to you.* Imagine the goodness of God being poured into your life. Imagine His joy filling you and His love flowing into you and through you. Imagine a life in the favour of the God who created you and loves you. Imagine being one with Him.

Please turn the page for exercises specific to your situation.

For Single People

Reflect

How can I love others with the extravagant love of Christ?

Could I be perfectly fulfilled as the bride of Christ if God called me to remain single?

What would my life look like as the bride and glory of Jesus Christ?

If I had to be single my entire life, can I imagine entering heaven feeling the regret of not having experienced earthly marriage?

Am I limiting the flow of God's goodness into my life or through me?

Pray

Lord, it is so awesome that you want to display your goodness to me. Thank you that I am your glory. I want you to be free to be extravagant with me. Please break off any limitations I have placed on You. Let your goodness and blessing flow into my life in such abundance that people will stand in awe of your goodness toward me. Let my life radiate an incredible love that brings you great glory.

Write

Father, I thank you that you are always making me more beautiful for Jesus. How would you like to make me more beautiful today?

For Husbands

Reflect

What does it mean for me to love my wife as Christ loves her?

How would my marriage change if I let Jesus love my wife through me?

Do I want to love my wife extravagantly? If so, how would that look today?

What would it take to make this kind of love sustainable long-term?

Pray

Jesus, thank you so much for calling me to be your bride. I offer you my marriage and ask that you would bring us into your design for marriage. Thank you for giving my wife to me. Please help me to know just how precious she is to you. Please share your heart for my wife with me. Love her through me. Serve her through me. Let your goodness be poured out upon her. May she experience your beauty in every aspect of her life. Please wrap her in your presence and clothe her in your splendour. Immerse her in your life and glory. May she be one with you and radiate with your perfect love, joy and glory.

Write

Jesus, how do you want to love my wife through me today?

For Wives

Reflect

What does it mean for me to be the glory of my husband?

Is there anything in me that would resist or reject his love?

Can I see the Spirit of Jesus within my husband?

What is God's vision for my marriage?

Am I willing to fight for God's design for my husband and our marriage?

Pray

Jesus, thank you so much for calling me to be your bride. I offer you my marriage and ask that you would bring us into your design for marriage. Thank you for giving my husband to me. Please help me to know just how precious he is to you. Please share your heart for my husband with me. Love him through me. Serve him through me. Let every barrier to love and intimacy within our marriage be completely removed. May I see you within my husband and love you through Him. May our marriage truly shine with your awesome love and brilliant joy.

Write

Jesus, how do you want to love my husband through me today?

For Married Couples

Ask each other some of the following questions:

Are you carrying any pain or unforgiveness towards me?

Are you carrying any pain or unforgiveness towards yourself?

Have we made any agreements with the enemy concerning our marriage?

Are you currently experiencing any rejection, dishonour, disrespect, anger, fear, hopelessness, control or manipulation in our marriage?

How can we make our marriage stronger?

What do you need right now? How can I help meet that need?

Do we see ourselves as a "we" unit, or as separate units of "you" and "I"?

Are we willing to fight together against pride, blame, accusation, offence and selfishness in our marriage?

Are we willing to embrace each other's successes and failures as one?

Are we free to live in the light with each other?

Do you feel like you can trust me enough to tell me anything without the fear of rejection or accusation?

What do you think the true me is like? Do you see the real me? Will you help me become the real me?

What do you think the true you is like? Do you see the real you? Will you let me help you become the real you?

Am I your first love after Jesus?

Pray
Write a prayer that you both fully agree with and are willing to act on together.

For People in Spiritually Unequal Marriages

"God I cannot stand this woman." For almost a year I spent a lot of time with a group of people, one of whom was a woman who had a broken past. As a child she was betrayed by her father, and as an adult she seemed to hold a deep-seated hatred of men. It was exhausting dealing with her day after day, so I took the situation to God.

"I've given her to you as a nail," the Lord responded, "...to keep you pinned to the cross." I could almost hear Him smile.

His words changed everything. Instead of seeing this woman as a source of attack, I realised that she was helping me to stay dependent on God. I started to let her words pass through me to the cross. I then started thanking God for her, knowing that she was helping me more than anyone else to cultivate a greater level of humility and intimacy with God.

If your spouse does not share the same heart for God or if they are unsupportive or difficult, be encouraged. God can use your spouse to help you to grow spiritually. They can spur you on to dependence. But the key is always to hear His voice. Marriage is a journey and there are simply no principles that can replace His voice of wisdom and love. If you continue to take time to listen to God, He will be faithful to speak to you and give you the grace you need to obey His voice.

Many people find themselves trapped in a marriage they feel undermines their calling in God. But know this: No one, no matter how disqualified or trapped they may feel, no one is ever exempt from the first command. There is no other call in life outside this call to first love. So if you make the first command your vision, it will be impossible for your spouse to get in the way. Why? Because God Himself promises to do everything it takes to bring you into the reality of wholehearted love.[2] Your spouse cannot stop the flow of God's love into you or through you. And the great news is that the best life you could ever live is found in the first command. Therefore, no matter who you have married, you will always have access to a life of wholehearted love and joy. Once the first command is in first place, God can help you to share His love for your spouse.

26. Aligned to Design

Reflect

Have I been submitting to the selfish nature in myself or in my spouse?

How can I actively submit to God's design for my marriage?

Am I ready to let go of my pride and control?

What does it mean for me to fight for our marriage?

Write

Write down any strongholds that you see by observation in your own life and that of your family. Ask God where the permission came from for these strongholds. Ask Him to expose the lies and replace them with His truth. Then pray something like this prayer:

Father, in Jesus' name I break the power of these lies in my life. I repent for believing these lies. I break every agreement with every spirit that has been made through these lies and I call every stronghold of the enemy in my life and in my marriage to be completely destroyed by the blood of Christ. I invite you to build a stronghold of your love and presence in my life and my marriage. Let us live in wholehearted love and truly become your glory.

Imagine

1 John 5:4
For everyone who has been born of God overcomes the world. And this is the victory that has overcome the world—our faith.

Romans 8:37 (NASB)
But in all these things we overwhelmingly conquer through Him who loved us.

Imagine God speaking to you and infusing your heart with the faith to overcome. Imagine your words carrying the power to break agreements and bring down strongholds. Imagine what it feels like to conquer your enemy and experience an overwhelming victory. Ask God to make it a reality.

27. To Love and Obey

Reflect

Am I obeying the call to love?

How can I love Jesus through His people?

What would that look like?

Do I feel like Jesus shares my needs?

Write

Lord, is there someone that I can love you through today?

Imagine

Matthew 6:31-33

"Therefore do not be anxious, saying, 'What shall we eat?' or 'What shall we drink?' or 'What shall we wear?' For the Gentiles seek after all these things, and your heavenly Father knows that you need them all. But seek first the kingdom of God and his righteousness, and all these things will be added to you."

Imagine Jesus saying these words to you. Imagine Him promising to provide all your basic needs for the rest of your life. Imagine being completely set free from all stress, anxiety and fear. Imagine Him sharing His sacrificial love with you and feel it filling your heart. Imagine Him taking your hand and leading you to someone who needs your love.

28. Believe and Love

Reflect

Which is more important to me: faith or love?

Am I willing to join or start a small group of people who are committed to loving God and each other?

If I am already in a small group, am I willing to share the message of love with the others?

As a group, could we commit ourselves to love?

Write

Lord, what is your vision for our fellowship?

Imagine

1 Peter 1:22 (BSB)
Since you have purified your souls by obedience to the truth so that you have a genuine love for your brothers, love one another deeply, from a pure heart.

1 Peter 4:8 (BSB)
Above all, love one another deeply, because love covers over a multitude of sins.

Imagine the Spirit of Jesus washing your soul. Imagine Him filling your heart with His genuine, unforced, selfless love. Imagine loving others *deeply*, having a love that sees past the sin and corruption, to behold the presence of Christ within His people. Imagine inspiring people to embrace their design of love and to find freedom from their selfishness. Imagine being part of a group of people who gather together, above all, just to love one another.

29. Bride Arise

Reflect

How can I grow in my obedience to God?

How can I exercise my authority in Christ?

Am I ready for a battle? Am I ready to contend for love?

Is my life bringing glory to God?

Write

Lord, are you calling me to connect with others in the net?

Imagine

Psalm 72:19
Blessed be his glorious name forever;
  may the whole earth be filled with his glory!
Amen and Amen!

Imagine the whole earth covered with small groups who love one another. Imagine the glory these groups would bring to the world. Imagine being in one of these groups and sharing each other's needs, knowing that you are part of a great net that will come together to meet your need. Imagine never having to worry about having need ever again. Imagine being free to love extravagantly.

30. Freely Give

Reflect

What is my next step in becoming the bride of Christ?

Is there anyone I can share this message of love with?

Am I willing to help others to prepare as a bride for Jesus?

Is God calling me to lead a group of people to prepare the bride?

Write

Father, how can I help to prepare your bride?

Would you like me to share this book with anyone?

Would you like me to support any of the projects mentioned in this book?

Imagine

Ephesians 3:20-21
Now to him who is able to do far more abundantly than all that we ask or think, according to the power at work within us, to him be glory in the church and in Christ Jesus throughout all generations, forever and ever. Amen.

Imagine a life of wholehearted love, intimacy and unity with Jesus. Imagine living in the fullness of your design of love. Now imagine God making it a reality. Imagine Him doing far more in you than you are presently daring to think or imagine. Imagine God receiving all the glory of your life of love.

About the Author

My name is Geoff (pronounced "Jeff") and I am an author, speaker, and founder of the Freeslaves.org project. I live in Dunedin, New Zealand, with my wife Melanie and our four children.

I started following Jesus as a child, but it was not until my early twenties that I began to come out of legalism and into the grace of His awe-inspiring love. I now live to love Jesus. He has done more in my life than I could ever express, and I pray He will always be my reason, my passion, my vision, and my goal.

Jesus says that Scripture depends on the commands to love God and love others. In the *One with Christ* series of books, I do my best to interpret the Scriptures through this lens of love in dependence on the Holy Spirit. If I have fallen short of this in any way, I ask you for your grace to look past any imperfections and to see the goal of the book, which is:

- To help you to prepare yourself as a bride for Jesus,
- To help you die to all legalism,
- To help you find your full delight in loving Jesus and being one with Him in covenant love.

I cannot express the privilege it is to have been able to invest in your journey into love and unity with Jesus. If you have come to know Jesus as your Bridegroom and would like to share your testimony with others, please email bride@onewithchrist.org. If you would like to learn more, ask a question, or simply connect with me, please visit onewithchrist.org.

All blessings and love in Christ,

Reference Notes

Introduction

[1] If you are not quite ready to read this book, relax. We are on a journey, so take your time, listen for His voice and simply focus on your next step. Know that the God of love is calling you and He will lead you into your inheritance in His perfect timing.

[2] At the outset, you may want to ask God if there are other people who can do this book with you and keep spurring you on to love. If there are, at the end of the book we have reflections for each chapter that can also be used for group study. Some people have gone through it by reading a chapter each week and then meeting to share their experiences with one another and pray together. Alternatively, we have specific group study guides available at onewithchrist.org. Simply be led in love.

1. Design of Love

[1] 1 Timothy 6:11, 1 Corinthians 1:30-31, Jeremiah 23:5-6

[2] Ephesians 4:2, Matthew 11:28-30

[3] 1 Peter 1:22

[4] 1 Peter 1:15-16, Hebrews 12:10

[5] Their names have been changed to protect their identities.

2. Channels of Love

[1] Some people may struggle at first by the notion that people are created as channels of God's love rather than individuals who are complete in themselves. Yet, Scripture says that Jesus is the image of God and we are created in His image (2 Corinthians 4:4, Colossians 1:15, Genesis 1:27). This means that we can only become who God created us to be when we come into union with Him and begin to share His heart. Apart from Christ we will never be complete, instead, we will be a channel for the selfish nature, which is not our true identity.

When we look the nature of people, we can see that we have always been channels. The parable of the Sower describes our lives as a field. When we are born, our brains are like unsown ground. All through life we let thoughts and ideas be sown into our hearts, and we have then expressed these thoughts through our words and actions. In this sense, we are effectively channels for the seeds that we let take root in our hearts. Through the parable of the Sower, Jesus invites us to let Him sow His seed in our hearts.

² Later in this book I share my testimony of what it feels like to have the Father's love for Jesus flow through us. However, I would love to encourage you to join with the Holy Spirit and seek the reality for yourself. If you feel led, please share your experiences with us at feedback@onewithchrist.org. It would be wonderfully encouraging to hear how the Father shares His love for Jesus with you.

³ See Matthew 1:21. God told Joseph to give Jesus his name because it means Yehovah (or Yahweh) saves, and Jesus came to save us from our sin. See also 1 Samuel 25:23-25 where Nabal's nature reflects his name. Even in modern language we still use a person's name to refer to their character or reputation.

3. Unique in Love

¹ The first command is like a military standing order. It is always in force, regardless of conditions or circumstances.

² *What's so Amazing About Grace?*—Philip Yancey, 1997, p71.

4. Value in Love

¹ This takes into account not working on the Sabbath and time off to observe the Jewish holy days.

² Colossians 2:13-14

³ Note in Isaiah 9:6, Jesus is referred to as the "Mighty God."

⁴ John 17:20-26

5. Into our Inheritance

¹ HELPS Word Study #1097

² HELPS Word Study #225

³ We need to remind ourselves that we are not the Holy Spirit and that we cannot bring ourselves into the reality of God's love or any other aspect of our spiritual inheritance through our own efforts. It is God's work and He wants to do it. All He wants is our permission and participation.

⁴ 2 Timothy 2:24-26

⁵ Luke 24:13-32

⁶ Note that the Greek word translated in Romans 10:17 as *word* is *rhema*, meaning "a spoken word by a living voice." See HELPS Word Study #4487.

⁷ Gift from God: Ephesians 2:8-9. Fruit of the Spirit: Galatians 5:22 (note that *faithfulness* is a mistranslation of the Greek word *pistis*, which means *faith*). For more on faith, please see onewithchrist.org/faith

⁸ See onewithchrist.org/faith for more detail on faith as the foundation for reality.

⁹ It is easy to mishear God so we need to be confident in testing His voice according to the standard of Scripture and the witness of the Spirit. Does the word convey a sense of spirit and life? Does it help us to love God and love others more? Does it affirm our unity with Jesus? We can also ask God for two or three independent witnesses (2 Corinthians 13:1) and find wisdom in getting feedback from some trusted counsellors who are also seeking their design of love (Proverbs 11:14). Please see *First Love* for more on hearing and testing the voice of God.

6. You Alone

¹ God is not only loving, He is love. He is not only good, but He is goodness itself. The very maximal expression of every good quality is found in God. Because His love and goodness are both perfect and infinite, we will never be able to imagine just how loving and good God truly is. This gives us permission to engage our imagination and to go to the limits. We can feel safe in the knowledge that whatever we imagine the ultimate extreme of love and goodness to be, we will still not be able to capture their true fullness in God.

² See John 3:16, 1 John 4:7-12, 2 John 1:9, Ephesians 1:3

³ Lord (John 13:13), Savior (Philippians 3:20), King (1 Timothy 6:13-16), Father (Romans 8:15), Mother (Luke 13:34), Brother (Matthew 12:46-50), Master (Matthew 23:8-12), Savior (1 Timothy 4:10), Judge, (2 Timothy 4:1-2), Teacher (John 13:13), Healer (Acts 9:34, Isaiah 53:5, Exodus 15:26), Counselor (Isaiah 9:6), Shepherd (John 10:16), Helper (John 14:26), Protector (2 Samuel 22:3), Provider (Matthew 6:25-34), Friend (John 15:13-15).

All of these relationships are like the different facets of a diamond. As the light of Christ shines through the diamond, we discover a glorious array of colors through the different facets of each relationship; each one expressing a different light of His radiant love, and each one bringing its own glory and blessing to our lives. If we focus only on one relationship, we deny ourselves the amazing beauty of God that is revealed through the other relationships. Let us continue to press on and know our God in all these depths!

⁴ Note that the greatest love we can have is to lay down our life for Christ. This does not only mean that we need to be prepared to physically die for Jesus. Our present life is made up of time, relationships, and possessions. If we want to know Jesus as a friend, we need to continually lay these down before Him as an offering to be used for His love and glory.

⁵ For more study, please read *First Love*, where we look at this in terms of legalism and grace.

⁶ See Galatians 3:26, 4:6, Romans 8:14-19, Hebrews 12:7.

7. A Time for Love

[1] In *First Love,* we saw how Scripture defines life as the state of a wholehearted love for God and union with Him. Spiritual death is therefore the state of selfish isolation. See Deuteronomy 30:6 and Luke 10:25-28 where Scripture defines life as loving God with all our heart and soul. We look at this more in the *First Love* book.

[2] The precise meaning of *El Shaddai* is debated, but some scholars believe it to be "The God of the Breasts" in the sense of the God who nurtures and cares for us. Other meanings include "The All Sufficient God" or "God of the mountains."

[3] This process of maturity is intimately connected with our sense of identity. During our early years of natural life, we look to our parents to define our identity as we learn about who we are and discover our place within our family. This is also true spiritually. As children of God, we look to our Father in heaven to define our identity and our place in His family. He does this through His Spirit and His word. When the Spirit breathes upon the Scriptures, they become a window through which we can see God, and a mirror that shows us who we are in union with Him (James 1:22-25). Every command in the word of God gives us a revelation of our true identity in Christ. Every teaching of Scripture draws us deeper into our design of love. This makes the word of God is so much more than just a set of ancient writings. It is a living and active revelation of God and the life we can have in Him, and as such is a key to maturing in Christ.

[4] Romans 5:1-2. Ephesians 2:8-9

[5] Note the Hebrew word *kanaph* literally means *wing,* but it is also used to refer to the edge or corner of a garment. Therefore some translations read, "*spread your covering*" or "*spread the corner of you garment,*" however, these translations obscure the idiom of marriage as coming under the wing of the husband.

8. Covenant of Love

[1] See Deuteronomy 6:1-5. *This is the commandment…You shall love the Lord your God with all your heart and soul.* In Matthew 22:34-40, Jesus says that all the Law and Prophets (meaning all of Scripture) depend or hang on this command and the command to love others as ourselves. The whole Law was simply a call to love.

[2] In traditional Jewish culture, once this covenant was made, it was binding to both bride and groom—only death or divorce could break off the engagement.

9. One with Christ

[1] See Romans 6:1-11, Galatians 5:16-24, Ephesians 2:3

[2] Philippians 1:21

10. Preparing for Love

1 Revelation 8:3-4

2 Strong's Hebrew Lexicon #08562

3 In the New King James Version, the word *tamruq* is translated as "preparations for beautifying women."

4 See 1 Corinthians 3:1-3

5 See *And He Will* (book three of the *One with Christ* series) for more on the awesome power of the blood of Christ.

6 Hebrews 3:13

7 Psalm 19:12

11. Ten Virgins

1 We will look at this, and other objections to knowing Jesus as our bridegroom in Chapters 21 and 22.

2 Matthew 4:17

3 See also Luke 5:33-35

4 Note that because Jesus does not reveal the clear meanings of the symbols He uses in this parable, any interpretation will be subjective and should be treated as such. The author expects that some people will interpret these symbols in different ways.

5 See also 1 Samuel 16:13. The Spirit of God came upon David as he was anointed with oil. See also Luke 4:18-19, where Jesus is anointed with the Spirit of the Lord.

6 Luke 2:29-32

7 See onewithchrist.org/revelation for more on revelation.

8 See also John 14:16-17, 1 John 3:24, 1 John 4:16

9 See onewithchrist.org/presence for more on developing this kind of relationship with the Spirit of Jesus.

10 Job 22:22, Hebrews 8:10

11 Deuteronomy 29:29. See onewithchrist.org/revelation for more on light and revelation.

12. Love and Humility

1 It is noted that there is debate concerning whether the universe is finite or infinite.

2 Matthew 22:35-40

3 Hebrews 11:6

4 HELPS Word Study # 4336. See Chapter 30 of *First Love* for more on prayer.

5 For those who are interested, God spoke further saying "I will fix the problem but it won't be by a miracle and it won't bring Me glory." And so it was. God was so

gracious to restore the data through a data recovery service, but He received no glory for the restoration.

6 This group only ran for six weeks or so. Yet it inspired me in the word of God and set me in a direction that would shape my spiritual life. Thank you to Ross Thompson for taking the time to spend a few evenings with a handful of students. It has made a world of difference to me.

13. Undistracted Devotion

1 We look at worship in more detail in *First Love* and at onewithchrist.org/worship.

2 The Bible often speaks about the importance of song and calls us to praise and celebrate God in singing. Singing is good and an important part of our spiritual growth. However, the reality is that our singing typically costs us little more than our time. Because it has no cost, singing does little to cultivate humility in a believer's heart, which means that singing is not often a true expression of worship. It is interesting to note that in the Psalms, the word *praise* outnumbers the word *worship* by ten-to-one.

3 2 Samuel 24:24

4 Another way that Scripture uses this technique is through the historical present tense, which describes a past action in its present form. Most English translations render the historical present in the past tense for readability, though the Discovery Bible and the New American Standard use the asterisk (*) symbol to mark where the historical present is used.

14. Dying to the Law

1 The same principle applies in our friendships. When someone tries to earn our friendship by trying to do or say the right things, there is something within us that naturally recoils. We know that love cannot be earned. Friendship cannot be earned. To pour out love in response to a person's works denies the nature of love as a free gift.

2 It is interesting to note that all the gods of this age demand works and sacrifice in return for a blessing. God only asks that we have the faith to receive the free gift of His love and grace.

3 Ezekiel 23

4 See Revelation 18:1-8 and Isaiah 52:1-12. Note that in 2 Corinthians 6:14-18, Paul quotes this passage to come out of legalism. He says that believers cannot be unequally yoked with leaders who teach legalism. Just as light has no fellowship with darkness, so grace cannot be joined to legalism, nor a living faith to dead works.

15. Leaving the Vineyard

[1] When the Hebrew canon of Scripture was decided upon, the Song of Songs was included solely on the basis of its symbolism of the romance between God and His people.

[2] See also Psalm 80:8 and Hosea 9:10.

[3] For passages on bringing joy to God see Isaiah 62:4-5, Zephaniah 3:17

[4] Hebrews 6:10

16. Sarah Must Die

[1] Hebrews 11:19

[2] See onewithchrist.org/types for more on types and realities.

17. Let Him

[1] Yadayim, Chapter 3, Mishnah 5.8

[2] 1 Thessalonians 5:8

[3] In Scripture the neck often speaks of the will. When God called Israel a stiff-necked people in Exodus 32:9, it spoke of their stubborn refusal to yield to His will. See also Acts 7:51.

[4] We will look at these and other objections in detail in Chapters 21 and 22.

18. With One Look

[1] See Chapter 2. We also look at this in more detail in Chapter 33 of *First Love*.

19. Seeking out the Bride

[1] John 6:1-13

20. Eunuchs for the Kingdom

[1] See HELPS Word Study #2135 and Thayer's Greek Lexicon, NT 2135.

21. Bride or Babe?

[1] Faith accesses grace (Romans 5:1-2) and acts in love (Galatians 5:6). God energises us to act according to His will (Philippians 2:13).

[2] Note that Scripture says that the grace of God worked through Paul to energise him to work more than all the other apostles (1 Corinthians 15:10). When the grace of God works, it works hard.

[3] This teaching neglects the first command, for by claiming that everyone is already in the covenant of the bride, it is saying by extension, *All of us are already loving God with all our heart, mind, soul, and strength. We just need to believe it.* This

makes no sense. The only way to love God with our entire being is by devoting our entire being to love. This is a conscious decision that does not happen without our consent.

4 The emphasis on belief over relationship makes little sense. It is like trying to convince the bride to believe she is beautiful without doing anything to make her beautiful. Or it is like raising up soldiers by telling them how great they are at fighting, but doing nothing to train them for battle. The intention is good, but the foundation is flawed.

5 Or someone who has been recently married.

6 Song of Solomon 2:7

7 If someone wants to argue about the bride from this perspective, simply direct them to God and to the first command. As He did for the Laodiceans, God will tell someone where they are spiritually, and how they can grow. You can say, "Just ask Him about it. Let Him speak. He will tell you if you have already come to know Jesus as your husband. He'll talk about the unity that you share with Jesus. He will confirm that you have devoted your life to loving Him with all your heart, soul, mind and strength. (You have done that right? Great!) So don't be afraid to ask Him. Let Him shape your theology and your faith."

22. Bride to Be?

1 This is just a select list where God is explicitly described as a husband to His people. In many other places it is stated implicitly. Hosea 2:7, 14-20; Isaiah 54:5, 62:3-5; Ezekiel 16:8-14, Jeremiah 31:31-33, Ephesians 5:25-33, 2 Corinthians 11:2.

2 We live out our present lives in the world. The phrase "so that the world may know…" places the focus of Jesus' prayer squarely in the present lifetimes of Jesus' followers. He is praying to the Father for His bride, that we would become one with Him in love in our present lives.

3 1 Corinthians 11:27-32, 2 Corinthians 13:5, John 7:24, 1 Peter 4:17

4 The present-day judgment of God separates good from evil within our own lives and is an expression of His great love. When God passes judgment, He then consumes what is evil within us and brings us into a greater level of purity and freedom. See Isaiah 4:4, where the Lord washes away the filth from the daughters of Zion and makes them clean by a spirit of judgment and of burning.

5 Psalm 35:13

6 Revelation 19:8

7 Ezekiel 44:17-18

8 Ephesians 6:13-17

23. Redeeming the Bride

1 In the context of 1 John, the test was to see if the teaching affirmed that Jesus came in the flesh (which aligns with Scripture). At the time, there were teachers who taught that Jesus did not have a physical body but was only a spirit. This was a teaching known as *Gnosticism,* which viewed the spiritual as entirely good and physical matter as entirely evil. Therefore Jesus did not have a body (which is evil) but rather was a spirit (which is good). John refutes Gnosticism in his letters.

2 We look more at this in *First Love.*

3 As teachers, we must be able to answer that question. The best way to prepare is to ask ourselves often: where are the people in our sphere of ministry who have made a covenant of love with Jesus? How can we prepare more people for this realm of love?

24. Stretch and Grow

1 HELPS Word Study #1519

2 This is perfect in the sense of a completed (not ongoing) action, not in the sense of a pure (not defiled or mixed) action. Note also that the underlined words represent text that is emphasised in the original Hebrew.

3 The word *awake* is written in the Hebrew hiphil stem which extends the meaning of a word from a literal sense (qal) into a figurative (in this case spiritual) sense. The hiphil stem prompts the reader to ask "How is this happening?" In this verse we would ask "How is this awakening happening?" The answer is this spiritual awakening is brought about by hearing and treasuring the thoughts of God, and by appreciating the vast number of His affections. This was true for David and it is true for every believer.

4 1 Corinthians 2:9-16, John 16:13, Psalm 139:17-18.

25. Bride and Glory

1 Note that this promise for Jerusalem is directly relevant to us as it is ultimately fulfilled in the heavenly Jerusalem, which is also called the bride and wife of Christ (Revelation 21:9-11).

2 1 Corinthians 11:3

3 I later talked about it with him, and he was grateful for the correction.

26. Aligned to Design

1 See 1 Corinthians 13:1-8 and 2 Timothy 1:7. Power is secondary to love, and it is love that gives the supernatural manifestations of power their eternal value.

2 It goes against the selfish nature to give anything away for nothing. There are always strings attached, even in marriage. Yet love keeps no records of wrong—it is not interested in trying to balance the scales. I once had to go overseas for five weeks when our four children were all under 11 years old. Melanie looked after the children without a single offer of help the whole time I was away. When I arrived back she looked me in the eye and said, "You need to know, you owe me nothing." Her words freed me from any sense of debt in the relationship and created a greater sense of unity in the relationship. Love keeps no records of wrong, and neither does it keep score.

3 Note that before verse 22, many translations insert a new heading in the text which disconnects it from the previous sentence which calls us all to submit to each other. Note also that the word *submit* is not present in the Greek in verse 22. Instead, it is implied from the previous sentence. For this reason, the Bible text has been edited to improve the flow between verse 21 and 22.

4 *Brown-Driver-Briggs Hebrew and English Lexicon*, referenced on the website: https://biblehub.com/hebrew/5048.htm

5 Deuteronomy 33:26,29, Psalm 33:20, 70:5, 115:9-11

6 See Colossians 2:11 and the next book in the series, *And He Will*.

27. To Love and Obey

1 In Psalm 27, David speaks of beholding the beauty of the Lord in His tabernacle. One way of beholding the beauty of God is to meditate on His nature. To do this, we can take an aspect of His nature, such as His goodness or love or faithfulness or joy, and then go to the very limits of our imagination. As we imagine the nature of God in the very extreme of our imagination, even there we fall short of envisioning the true nature of God. He is better than we could ever imagine. He is more loving than we could ever dream. So let us be free to extend the limits of our imagination, so that we might behold His beauty with greater clarity and appreciation.

2 Note that this prayer goes on to ask for daily bread. This is not simply having enough physical food for the day, but hearing His voice, which is like bread for our soul. We then ask forgiveness for our debts. As we learned earlier, our debt to God and people is one of love. Where we have failed to love, we need forgiveness. We also need to forgive others for not loving us. This forgiveness will help to fortify our hearts against the enemy. Lead us not into temptation; especially the temptation to withhold our love. Deliver us from evil; be our shelter from the enemy and keep us from making any agreements with him. For Yours is the kingdom, power and glory forever.

When put together, we find the pattern of this prayer is:

- Affirming our relationship and identity
- Remembering the nature of God
- Aligning our will with the will of God
- Thanking God for provision and inviting intimacy
- Receiving forgiveness for our ongoing debt of love
- Seeking protection from the enemy
- Declaring the eternal majesty and dominion of God!

[3] 1 Timothy 1:5 (NASB)

[4] John 20:30-31

[5] See John 17:26. Jesus continues to reveal the Father's name to us so that:

1. The Father's love for Jesus could live in us; and
2. Jesus Himself could live within us.

These two goals reveal our ultimate design. As channels of the Father's love for Jesus, we can love Him through one another because Jesus lives within His people. Together, we are all a part of the divine flow of love.

28. Believe and Love

[1] 1 John 3:14

[2] If the only fellowship we experience is at a Sunday service and we know we cannot love a crowd, then we need to ask ourselves: are we truly obeying the call of love?

29. Bride Arise

[1] Colossians 3:14

30. Freely Give

[1] See Ezekiel 16:48-49

[2] James 2:5

Small Groups

[1] The first four questions have been taken from John Wesley's guidelines for small groups.

Study Guide

[1] See *First Love* for more on receiving revelation from God.

[2] Deuteronomy 30:6

CONE WITH CHRIST

Visit www.onewithchrist.org for the next book
in the *One with Christ* series.

Made in the USA
Monee, IL
06 February 2023

26483984R00148